TOTAL TENNIS

A Guide to the Fundamentals of the Game

TOTAL TENNIS

A Guide to the Fundamentals of the Game

Hana Mandlikova and Betty Stove

SIMON SCHUSTER

AUSTRALIA

Note
For simplicity and clarity this book is presented from Hana
Mandlikova's perspective. It has, however, been co-authored with
Betty Stove and the approach to tennis belongs to both.

The rules of tennis are reproduced and slightly abridged with kind
permission of the New South Wales Tennis Association from *Rules
of Tennis, Official Book of the Australian Lawn Tennis Umpires'
Association*.

TOTAL TENNIS

First published in Australasia in 1990 by
Simon & Schuster Australia
7 Grosvenor Place, Brookvale NSW 2100

A division of Paramount Communications Inc.

© Hana Mandlikova and Betty Stove 1989

National Library of Australia
Cataloguing in Publication data

Mandlikova, Hana.
   Total tennis.
   Includes index.
   ISBN 0 7318 0066 4.
   1. Tennis. I. Stove, Betty. II. Title.
796.342

Cover photographs by Roger Gould
Designed by Helen Semmler
Illustrations by Colin Bodie Illustration
Typeset in Hong Kong by Setrite Typesetters Ltd
Printed in Australia by Globe Press Pty Limited

CONTENTS

FOREWORD

In 1977 I took the first Australian Junior Team to play in Czechoslovakia. The reason for that was twofold. Firstly, I believed that Czechoslovakia had a good tennis system and good players. Secondly, I was interested in the structure, training and the techniques used in their coaching system. It was rather ironic that in 1979 a young woman, Hana Mandlikova, made her first venture to Australia because it was here that she hoped to learn more about the game of tennis and consequently improve her game.

Total Tennis has some interesting tit-bits. These include Hana's first 'racquet' her father made from a piece of wood. Then there was the time in 1972 when Betty Stove teamed with Françoise Dürr to win the US Open Doubles in coloured clothing.

Total Tennis gives us an understanding of the rules of, for example, tie-break sets and time taken between points. Hana, from Czechoslovakia and Betty, from the Netherlands, have used training and coaching methods which are slightly different to that of Australia. Thus, they introduce us to their wealth of experience in relation to grips and technique and encourage you to play your strokes 'easy, smooth, well co-ordinated and relaxed'. You can imagine that if you do play your strokes in such a fashion and that you are very consistent, then you can have lots of fun and enjoyment by 'watching your opponent run and not yourself'.

And this is what *Total Tennis* is all about. Teaching you the 'total game' as a beginner to enjoy tennis. If you are a tennis lover, or even a fanatic, there are many hints in the book for you too.

Have lots of fun,

Denis Colette

DENIS COLETTE
Australian Director of Coaching

INTRODUCTION

Tennis is first and foremost a sport. In recent times, for many professional players, it seems to have become more like a business, and this is a trend we should all work against. Sport means fun and relaxation, and I think that is the most important part of tennis.

In my view, tennis instruction should begin at a young age, eight to thirteen years old. At this stage it is important that children get as much fun out of the game as possible, as that way they will improve. For this reason, they should be taught in groups, of preferably more than four, rather than on a one-to-one basis. Eventually, those who show promise can be given individual coaching.

For the individual, keep setting goals for yourself that are within your capacity, and practise with someone who has the same goals. The training program should be designed so that every person involved is able to enjoy the progress. Don't set goals that are too high. Rather, go step by step, because otherwise the pleasure goes out of it. Success will eventually come but it takes time.

For the beginner, who has everything to learn, it is very important to receive instruction that is skilled and motivated. After the basics have been established, different strokes can gradually be added. Much later, tactics can start to play a part, and these involve many factors besides merely hitting the ball. The better you become the more attention you should pay to details. These details may seem so insignificant but they can be worth so much.

When you practise, every shot should be executed with full concentration and balanced physical effort. One hour of practice like this may be twice as tiring but it will be ten times more valuable than many hours of mindless hitting.

Find out for yourself what is logical and what you can do, and don't always believe what others say. You are the one who has to execute the shot. Of course you must, if you want to improve, use the help of skilled people. But never become an unthinking slave.

Above all else, drive and determination will contribute most to your improvement. No matter how much excellent instruction you receive, it is still up to you to learn to use what is offered. And training for improvement demands total involvement and dedication. Success comes in small doses and unfortunately the better you get the more difficult it becomes. Improvements in tennis don't always go in a continuous upward motion. They are normally followed by a standstill or even a decline. Such periods can be very depressing. They often come when you are trying to do something in a new way, and time is needed to absorb the changes. It is so easy to find the energy and time to practise when things are going well, and equally, it is so easy to go to the movies or a disco when the going on the court is tough. It is at these times that the potential champion shows his or her true character. No one will deny that the best way to improve is to spend time on the court. But you also need time for the brain to absorb the points you are learning. And learning is as much a mental process as a physical process.

There are four elements that go to make a good tennis player: technique; physique; tactics on the court; and mental attitude. I believe the most important of these is the last, mental attitude.

NOTE: Without intending any bias towards righthanded players or to male players, at times, to avoid extremely convoluted directions, it has been necessary to use the terms 'left' and 'right' as they would apply to a righthanded player, and to use the terms 'he' and 'his' even though the content applies to both male and female players. In the former cases left-handed players should reverse the lefts and rights and instructions have usually been given to that effect.

A BRIEF HISTORY

The origins of tennis can be traced as far back as the ancient Romans. They used to play a game called trigon, using a paddle and a heavy ball made out of fig seeds. More recently, in the eleventh century, the Italians played a game called *gioco del pallone*. This had three to four members on each team, and was played against the outside walls of high buildings. *Jeugo de pelota* is a Spanish version of the game, and to this day it remains the Basque national sport. The size of court used depends on the number of players, who use beak-shaped paddles called chiestre.

In France, in the fourteenth century, a game called *jeu de paume*, game with the palm, was popular. By the fifteenth century small wooden paddles had been developed, which were later improved with leather cord and gut strings. It is from the system that was used for scoring this game, that the current method of scoring tennis has been developed. In Old French, *une journée* meant 'a sports match', as well as 'a day', and the scoring system was based on the number of hours in a day, and the number of minutes in an hour. Each match consisted of twenty-four games, which in turn consisted of four winning rallies worth 15 points each. However, it was soon realized that when both sides were at 45 points each, it would be necessary to win two rallies as otherwise the game might be decided on luck. But the total would exceed 60 points and therefore also the number of minutes in an hour, so the score was changed to 40−all with 10 points being given for each winning rally. If there was a tie at 50 points all, the score would go back to 40−all. The game could only be won by winning two rallies in a row. It was the same with the game score. At twenty-three games all, it was necessary to win two games in a row, or the score would be lowered to twenty-two−all. As matches became too long, the number of games played was lowered to twelve and then later to six.

By the seventeenth century *jeu de paume* had become much more popular and had spread to central and western Europe where it was played at court and at the universities. It was now played outdoors and had become very competitive. It was played for the first time in England in the fifteenth century.

There is some dispute in the history books as to the origin of *jeu de paume's* modern name, 'tennis', but I believe the word comes from the French word *tenir*, 'to hold' or 'catch'. In 1875 the game became known as 'lawn tennis'. Points were counted as in real tennis, the English version of *jeu de paume*.

Originally, tennis was a rather boring game played mostly from the baseline, although players soon began to use different strokes. The volley and smash were first played by the Renshaw brothers in England in the 1880s. Discussions were held as to whether it should be allowed, but the idea that it would make the game more attractive persuaded the conservative English. The net was lowered to today's height of 91.4 centimetres (3 feet) in the middle, in 1877. In 1868 the All England Croquet Club was founded and in 1877 tennis became a club activity and the name changed to the All England Croquet and Lawn Tennis Club. The club tennis championships were first played in 1877 at Worple Road, Wimbledon, a suburb of London. The championships became known as 'Wimbledon' and by 1883 sixty-five other countries were sending competitors. Since that time the rules of tennis have changed only slightly.

The game, however, does continue to evolve. Currently under discussion are ways to avoid the dominance of the service. Suggestions include putting the service position back by 1 metre (3.3 feet), making the service court shorter, or giving the server only one serve.

BASIC REQUIREMENTS

THE TENNIS RACQUET

The most obvious first requirement is a tennis racquet and there are many kinds on the market. My father made my first racquet or rather bat, as it had no strings. He carved it out of a piece of wood and it was just big enough for me to hit balls against the living room wall. I was very happy with this bat and whenever my mother went out, my father would quickly remove a cupboard and the surrounding furniture, so that I had a little place to hit against the wall. The room was rather small, 3 by 4 metres (10 by 13 feet), and from the very beginning my aim had to be good. I could not afford to break anything as then my mother would have learnt our secret. Fortunately it took her a long time to find out.

When you are very small, it is difficult to handle a big racquet properly. I would recommend that if you start playing tennis at an early age, you should use a mini-racquet. Then between ten and twelve years, depending on your size, you can advance to a junior racquet.

Nowadays, the old-fashioned wooden racquet is becoming almost a collector's item. But it is a good idea to start with a wooden racquet because this will give you a better feel for the dynamics of the game. Later you can change to a more powerful racquet which will give you more speed.

Seniors will have to pay attention to three points when buying a new racquet.

1. The weight. Light, medium or heavy.
2. The grip size. This is usually measured from three to eight.
3. The kind of gut. Synthetic or real gut.

These days there are many materials used to make racquets. From boron to kevlar, from ceramic to fibreglass, and they all last a long time. A good racquet will last at least three years if you look after it. There is much discussion over which material is the best. Basically, the more flexible the racquet the more power you have, and the stiffer the frame the more control you have.

When you become a seasoned player you will develop your own preferences for one material or another, but remember, always try a new brand out before you invest so much money. Test the racquet. How does it feel in your hand? Does it feel comfortable, heavy, light? If you are a volley player you may like to have a slightly lighter racquethead. In general you should use an evenly balanced racquet, that is, if you balance the racquet in the middle the racquethead and handle should be of equal weight.

The Handle

When you wrap your fingers around the handle they should go round it easily. They should not overlap too much, and the nail of the thumb should sit nicely beside the nail of the middle finger and the forefinger.

In the early days, when racquets were all made of wood, there was often no grip on the handle. Players like Don Budge (first Grand Slam winner, 1938) preferred to feel the sharp edges of the wood as they maintained it gave a better feel in the hand. Nowadays, the handles of modern racquets are made of artificial material and a leather grip is required to protect and give the best feel in the hand.

The Strings

When you buy a racquet, the strings usually come with the sale. But if you should advance to the level of matchplayer, then it becomes important to have your racquet strung to suit your individual needs, and for this purpose you will need a very good stringer. Today, in the over-size racquets, players mainly use synthetic gut. It is cheaper and lasts longer. Only a handful of tournament players still use real gut, because in bad weather conditions it doesn't last long. Fortunately my sponsor supplies me with plenty.

Tension is an important aspect of stringing. When beginning, I suggest that you use the recommended tension for your size of racquet. However, if you become very advanced, you will find that different styles of play demand different tension. Bjorn Borg used a tension as high as 35 kilograms (77 pounds) because he played a lot of topspin, while John McEnroe sometimes plays with a tension as low as 17−18 kilograms (37−40 pounds) because he plays much flatter and needs the extra control. I use one between 25 and 29 kilograms (55 and 64 pounds), depending on the weather, brand of balls and court surface.

BALLS

Over the last twenty years balls have undergone quite a few changes. The weight, size, bounce and compression are now strictly regulated. For the matchplayer, the balls must have exactly the right weight, tension and temperature. The temperature of the air inside a ball should be about 15°C (60°F). If it is colder the ball will be slower and if hotter, the bounce will be unpredictable. The beginner, however, can use old or softer balls. Softer balls are easier to play with as they don't fly as hard and you will have more time to prepare. As with buying a tennis racquet, get advice from your trainer on what kind is the best for your game.

CLOTHES AND SHOES

For many decades white was the only approved colour for tennis attire. Then in the early seventies light pastel colours began to be allowed. In 1972 Françoise Dürr and Betty Stove won the US Open doubles in 'coloured' dresses.

Nowadays tennis clothes are available in many colours, from dark blue and black to bright red. However, the All England Lawn Tennis and Croquet Club, where the Wimbledon Championships are played, still forbids players to wear too much colour. The attire has to be predominently white.

For warmer weather I recommend white cotton clothes. They take perspiration better and will also keep you cooler under bright sunshine. An additional good buy is a tracksuit, especially for warming up and for putting on when you have finished playing. When the muscles are warm it is easy to catch a chill if you are not careful.

When buying new shoes, make sure they feel flexible in the right places especially under the ball of your foot. Test the amount of support they give when making a quick turn, and make sure you can't step out of the shoe. Look also for good inner soles and for the right profile of the outer sole. You may need a different kind of sole for different court surfaces. On clay you need better grip and therefore a deep profile sole. On smoother surfaces shallower soles are best and simple 'pimple' soles suit grass courts.

It is very important that neither shoes nor clothes restrict any movement. You should feel free to stretch, run and leap in any direction.

COURTS

Court Surfaces

Grass courts have been the traditional surface in many countries, including England and Australia. But the maintenance of grass is very expensive and these are gradually being replaced with artificial surfaces. The new National Tennis Centre in Melbourne has a surface called Rebound Ace. This is a rubberized surface, developed in Australia, which is easy on the body. However, when the weather is extremely hot it can burn through the soles of your tennis shoes. Also, as the temperature rises, the rubber gets softer and becomes more flexible, making the ball bounce higher.

In Europe, most of the courts have a red clay surface. These differ slightly from country to country. The French undersurface their courts differently and use a much finer powdered brick topping than the Germans or Italians. When I am playing in Paris I always go there early to give myself time to adjust to the different surface. Clay is generally a fairly slow surface. Patience is a good quality for clay court players because the exchanges are usually quite lengthy. On hard courts the serve is more of a deciding factor but the surface is harder on the body. The service is especially important on grass courts where the balls bounce fairly low. Grass is sometimes uneven so a good touch and flexibility are important.

Nowadays there are also many indoor facilities and new improved kinds of carpet surfaces are constantly being developed. Of course indoor courts have the advantages of no wind, and play never being cancelled due to bad weather.

Outdoors, hard court and artificial grass are now normal court surfaces. These surfaces need hardly any maintenance and last a long time.

As you can imagine, all these different surfaces make it difficult for professional players who sometimes have to play on different courts from week to week. The better a player's technique, the more quickly he or she will adjust to a new surface. For the beginner, a change in court surface should not make much difference, although it is interesting to see how it can change your game. However, at this stage, it is more important to concentrate on learning the correct technical skills.

Measurements of the Court

When learning any new sport, you should always begin by familiarizing yourself with the area in which you are going to play. When beginning tennis, take the time to walk around a court and get a feel for its dimensions. Try to gauge distances, for example from the net to the baseline, or one side to another. This will help you enormously, especially as you become more advanced, because it will give you a better idea of what you can do with the ball and how much room you have. The quicker you develop a sense of where you are on the court, the more comfortable you will be in play.

The tennis court has nine lines. The two outermost lines on the short sides of the rectangle are the baselines. It is from these that a player must serve. Parallel to these and cutting the rectangle in half is the net, over which the ball must be hit. The two outermost lines on the long sides of the rectangle mark the boundaries within which the ball must bounce when playing doubles (two players on each side of the net). Slightly inside those are the two long lines which mark the boundaries when playing singles (one player on each side of the net). Thus, when playing singles, the area within which the ball must bounce is narrower than that allowed for doubles.

When serving, the ball must land in one of the four equal areas on each side of the net, depending on which side of the court and net you are serving from. The right hand area is called the 'deuce-court' (you receive the deuce point on this side) and the left side is called the 'ad-court' (you receive the advantage point on this side). These areas are bounded by the

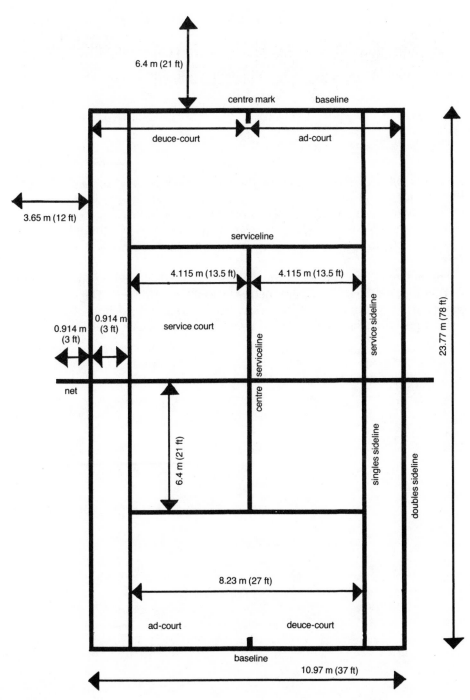

DIAGRAM 1

The standard tennis court.

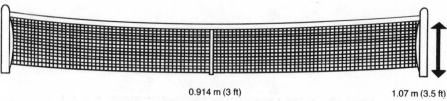

0.914 m (3 ft)   1.07 m (3.5 ft)

DIAGRAM 2

The net.

singles sideline or service sideline, the net, the centre serviceline (parallel to the sidelines) and the serviceline (parallel to the net).

In addition to the length of the court, beyond each baseline is a running area of at least 6.4 metres (21 feet); and in addition to the width of the court, beyond each doubles sideline is a running area of at least 3.65 metres (12 feet).

The height of the net, for both doubles and singles, is 91.4 centimetres (3 feet) in the middle and 106 centimetres (3.5 feet) at each end. The singles net posts are 91.4 centimetres (3 feet) away from the singles sidelines. In doubles the net posts are the same distance away from the doubles sidelines.

The Eastern grip

To get the Eastern grip take the racquet in the non-playing hand at the throat and place the playing hand flat on the strings.

Slide the playing hand down the racquet.

Keep sliding until the playing hand grips the handle.

The Continental grip

The Western grip

The backhand grip

The two-handed backhand grip

SCORING AND RULES
OF THE GAME

SCORING

Points in tennis are called love, 15, 30, 40, deuce and advantage.

The Game

O, or nothing, is called 'love'. It is believed to come from the pronunciation of the French word *l'oeuf*, which sounds like 'love'. The use of *l'oeuf*, meaning 'egg', to denote nothing, is derived from the shape of an egg. The first point won by a player is called 15, the second point, 30, the third point, 40. If a player then wins a fourth point before his opponent has won three points, then that player wins the game. However, if both players have won three points (40−all), the score is then deuce, and it is necessary to win two points in a row to win the game. The word 'deuce' comes from an Old French word, *deus*, meaning 'two'. The first point won after a score of deuce is called advantage, either to the server or receiver, but if that player loses the next point then the score returns to deuce. Here are the scores of two games in which deuce occurs:

15−love
15−all
30−15
40−15
40−30
deuce
advantage receiver (or player's name)
game receiver

In this game deuce occurred only once. Here is a game in which the score returned to deuce twice:

15—love
30—love
30—15
30—all
30—40
deuce
advantage server
deuce
advantage server
deuce
advantage receiver
game receiver

The Set

The first player who wins six games, wins the set, provided he has won two more games than his opponent. If the score reaches five games to six, then the winning player must win the next game. If the score reaches six games all, then it becomes a tiebreak (see the following section).

Men usually play the best out of five sets and women, the best out of three sets, except at the Virginia Slims Championships Finals in New York, where women play the best of five sets.

The Tiebreak

In most matches, when a game score of six—all is reached, a tiebreak is played. In a tiebreak the points are called 1, 2, 3, etc. Each side serves two points in a row, except at the beginning, when each side serves only once. This is so as not to give too great an advantage to the server. The player who wins the tiebreak game is the player who wins seven points with at least two more points than his opponent. He wins the set seven games to six. In a tiebreak the players must keep playing until one player is two points ahead.

In doubles the players serve alternately in the same order as before.

Change of Ends

The players change ends every time the total number of games played is uneven. This is so as not to give one player an advantage in outside conditions, such as wind or sun. This sometimes looks silly when tennis is played indoors, but those are the rules, and it also gives the players a chance to get some rest. In the tiebreak the players change ends after every six points.

Time between Points

The rulebook says play must be continuous, but it also says that you may take no longer than thirty seconds before playing the next point. Some match-players like to play cat and mouse with the opponent and stretch this rule to the utmost.

On the changeover the resting time is one minute. So as soon as the last point of the game is played, you will have ninety seconds before you have to start the next point.

On the Line

A ball that touches only a hair of the line is in, even if 99 per cent of the ball touches the ground outside the line. It goes without saying that this rule causes many disputes.

ETIQUETTE

Besides the rules of tennis there are also some important unwritten laws which come under the title of tennis etiquette. Tennis is a social game, a game involving simple politeness and consideration. Everyone will enjoy the game so much more if those standards are maintained. Here are some of the rules which I think are most important:

1. Always come prepared. Bring not only balls, but towels and water to drink when it is hot.
2. Never walk behind a court when a point is still in play. Wait until the point is over and then cross as fast as possible.
3. When sending balls back to a neighbouring court, roll them on to the back of the court. Never send them back while play is in progress.
4. Offer to bring new balls or organize a system to decide who brings the balls.
5. Retrieve balls for your partner and your opponent.
6. Don't criticize your partner, offer encouragement.
7. Call your own lines and let your opponent hear the call. If the ball is good say nothing and play on.
8. Always respect the linecalls of your opponent.
9. If there is a disagreement, offer a let. In other words, replay the point, even if it was a second service.

ROTATION AND
BOUNCE OF THE BALL

Before we discuss the actual playing of tennis I want to tell you a little about the rotation and bounce of the ball. There are four factors to take into account when considering the motion of the ball: the speed; the angle; the length and hop; and the direction.

SPEED OF THE BALL

The speed of the ball is determined by:
- The existing speed of the incoming ball.
- The power of the stroke.
- The kind of surface on which you are playing.
- The kind of stroke. A ball with topspin goes faster than a flat ball or ball with no spin. And a flat ball goes faster than a ball with underspin or slice. (The methods for giving a ball topspin or underspin are discussed on p. 40.)

ANGLE OF THE BALL

- The rebound of a topspin ball will be at a smaller angle to the horizontal after the bounce than before the bounce.
- The rebound of a flat ball will be at the same angle to the horizontal after the bounce.
- The rebound of an underspin ball will be at a larger angle to the horizontal after the bounce than before the bounce. And the more underspin it has, the higher the ball will bounce, to the extent that it can even return on itself. (See Diagram 4.)

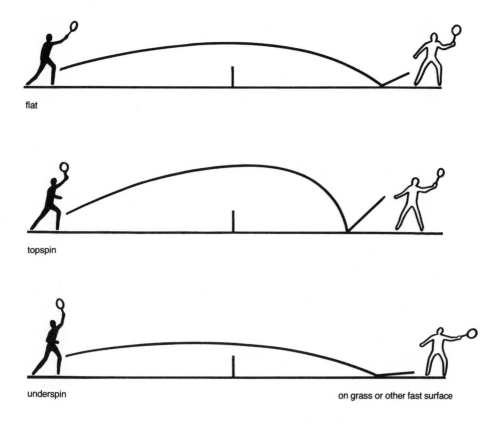

flat

topspin

underspin   on grass or other fast surface

DIAGRAM 3

Height of the ball.

LENGTH AND HOP OF THE BALL

Besides topspin, flat balls and underspin, we should also talk about the length and hop of the stroke. Imagine three balls hit with the same power and at the same angle. The topspin ball will have a shorter length but will jump further after the bounce. The ball with underspin will have more length but will not jump as far after the bounce. And the flat ball will do something in between.

Diagram 7 on page 25 shows three balls with the same height and length, and you can see the result of the different strokes. To achieve the same height and length the underspin ball has to be played with less power and the topspin with more power. But you can see again the angle of the different strokes after the bounce of the ball. Underspin short and topspin longer.

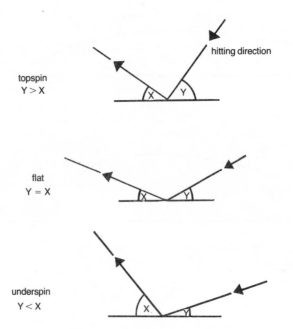

Angle of the ball.

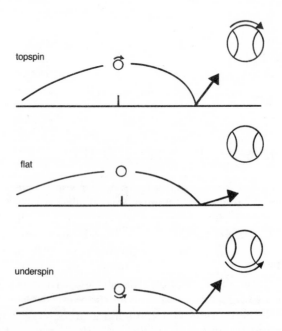

Height and bounce of the ball.

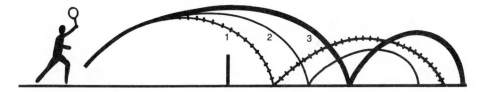

DIAGRAM 6

Length and hop of the ball.
1. *Topspin*
2. *Flat*
3. *Underspin*

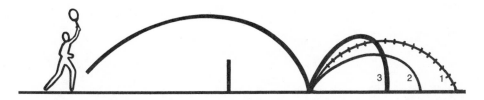

DIAGRAM 7

Height and bounce of the ball.
1. *Topspin*
2. *Flat*
3. *Underspin*

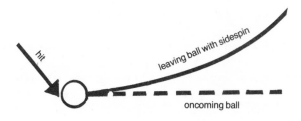

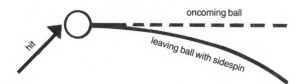

Sidespin.   *DIAGRAM 8*

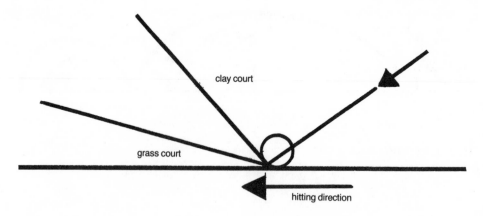

DIAGRAM 9

The ball's bounce on grass and clay surfaces.

DIRECTION OF THE BALL

There is one rotation I have not yet discussed and that is sidespin. With normal stroking, a ball with topspin, no spin or underspin, will move after the bounce in the same direction from which it came. With sidespin, however, the ball will move to the right or left depending on how you stroked the ball. (See Diagram 8.)

HOW SURFACE AFFECTS THE BALL

When the ball hits the court surface friction occurs, and of course different surfaces cause different amounts of friction. (See Diagram 9.)

The best surfaces for spins are the slower (rougher) surfaces because the friction is greater. On a fast surface there is less friction between ball and surface, meaning that spinning balls are given less power. The most effective shot on faster courts is the ball with underspin because its bounce is slow. This is not, as you might think, because of the underspin, but because of the lesser effect of the rotation and the lower flight of the ball over the net. A ball that is hit hard will skid much more at the bounce, especially on slower surfaces, and make a smaller angle when coming up.

BASIC SKILLS

GRIPS

Why are some players better than others? They can hit the ball more consistently, more powerfully and more accurately. Their base is well-balanced and their technique is correct. The grip, of course, is the beginning of good stroking. If you play with a grip or a stroke that worries you, you will have no confidence to 'go' for the shot you have in mind. Don't be afraid to change your grip. And remember, it is never too late to change. Tennis is a game that can be played for a lifetime. During my career, which is not yet that long, I have changed my forehand grip twice, and while it took a little while to adjust, I always felt it became better and better.

Your choice of grip is important because it decides your playing style. For example, if you have a grip which does not allow you to play a good smash or service you will probably become a defensive player, a player who prefers to stay on the baseline.

The mechanics of the Eastern and Continental grips are the easiest to learn. With these grips you can serve, hit groundstrokes, volley and smash. The Western grip is good for high bouncing surfaces and therefore suitable for many of the fast surfaces. Advice about the best grip to use varies considerably. More professional players are beginning to use the Western grip. For beginners, however, the Eastern and Continental grips can be beneficial and I recommend that you use either of these or something in between.

For the beginner, it is important to know the right grip for the stroke you are going to play. Learn it fast and you will improve quickly.

If you have played for a while, you will already have a grip, and it may be different from the ones I advocate. Don't change it if you have confidence in it. However, keep reading, you may find out something new that will help your game. On the other hand, if you feel you are not making any progress, you may have to change your grip somewhat. Make sure you get good advice before you do so.

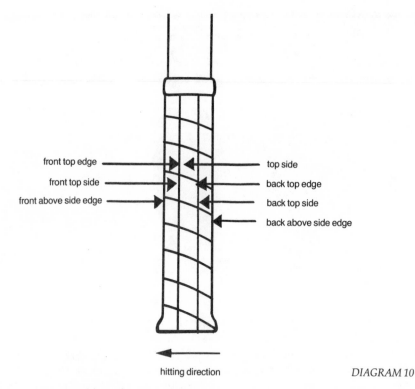

front top edge — top side

front top side — back top edge

front above side edge — back top side

back above side edge

hitting direction

DIAGRAM 10

The racquet handle viewed from above.

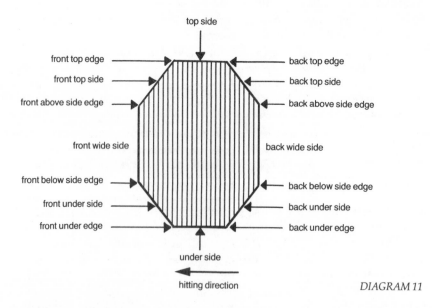

top side

front top edge — back top edge

front top side — back top side

front above side edge — back above side edge

front wide side — back wide side

front below side edge — back below side edge

front under side — back under side

front under edge — back under edge

under side

hitting direction

DIAGRAM 11

The racquet handle viewed from the end.

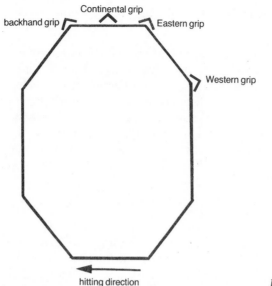

DIAGRAM 12

The racquet handle viewed from the end showing the position of the 'V' between index finger and thumb for the various grips.

Professional players all have different grips and therefore different styles. They also all have different physiques and different personalities. This is what makes the game of tennis so interesting to play, and to watch.

Eastern Grip
How to Get the Eastern Grip

The Eastern grip is also called the shake hands grip. Take the racquet in the non-playing hand, at the throat (just below the head), and hold it in front of your body. Place the playing hand flat on the strings with an open palm. Now slide it slowly down the racquet and shake hands with the handle. The V of the hand between forefinger and thumb should now be placed over the back top edge of the racquet with the thumb around the handle. Keep the hand relaxed and the fingers spread lightly.

Advantages
- The hand is spread right over the handle, giving good support to the wrist and allowing long contact with the ball.
- On the forehand the ball can be struck with an extended arm in front of the left hip (right hip for lefthanded players).

Disadvantage
- This grip is not normally used for the backhand, service or smash. On the backhand, the racquet would only be held by the ends of the fingers, and would receive no support from the wrist, and therefore have no power.

On the smash and service the hand would not be free to move swiftly forwards.

The Eastern grip is very good for the forehand and forehand volley. Some top players also use it for the backhand and for a flat service (*see p.43*), but I recommend that you use a different grip for the backhand, service (unless you are a beginner, when it can be quite useful) and smash. With the Eastern grip you can play an attacking game as well as a defensive game. The stroke has little lift or topspin which makes it a bit safer. When you want to you can even play a heavier topspin or a flat drive without changing your grip.

Continental Grip

This grip, named after the early European players, is also called the Universal grip, because it can be used for both forehand and backhand.

How to Get the Continental Grip
Hold the racquet out in front in the playing hand, with the racquethead perpendicular to the body. The hand should be relaxed and with the fingers slightly spread so that the V between forefinger and thumb falls over the top side of the racquet, right between the two top edges of the handle. The centre of the palm should rest on the back top side of the handle. Looked at from above, this grip should resemble an extension of the arm. A slight variation of this is the semi-Continental grip, in which the V between forefinger and thumb is placed a little further round, between the Continental grip and the Eastern grip.

Advantages
- The Continental grip allows you to play all shots without changing your grip. On faster courts this may help you to save time, especially at the net.
- The wrist has a more natural position for hitting low bouncing balls in front of the body and for getting the dropshot (*see p. 50*).
- On the backhand and backhand volley you can hit the ball in front of the right hip (left hip for lefthanded players).
- On the serve and smash, the wrist position is freer and can therefore give more power and snap to the stroke.

Disadvantages
- The Continental grip will not work well on the forehand unless the timing and pivot of the stroke are absolutely accurate.
- It is difficult to hit balls that bounce higher than the shoulder.
- A strong wrist and forearm are necessary for this grip.

I recommend using this grip for the backhand, backhand volley, service and smash.

Western Grip

How to Get the Western Grip
The easiest way to learn the Western grip is to place your racquet flat on the ground and then to pick it up. You will see now that the V between forefinger and thumb is placed over the back above the side edge.

Advantage
- This grip will help you on high bouncing balls. Because the wrist lies behind the handle, it gives you more power behind the shot.

Disadvantages
- It is very hard to get the racquethead under low bouncing balls.
- Because the racquethead is not open, on the volley the ball will ricochet into the net.

The Western grip can only really be used to advantage on the forehand, with high bouncing balls. However top players like Chris Evert and Guillermo Vilas use it for several strokes.

The Backhand Grip

How to Get the Backhand Grip
For the backhand grip, I recommend a slight variation on the Continental grip. Move the hand slightly further around the racquet so that the V between forefinger and thumb is now placed over the front top edge of the handle. That way you will have a good part of the ball of the thumb behind the racquet handle.

Advantages
- With this grip, the wrist will support the stroke well. The racquet will lie comfortably in the hand, with the fingers lightly spread.
- With the help of the other hand, you will be able to take the racquet back parallel to the ground and accelerate with a stretched arm through the stroke. Hit the ball well in front of the right hip (left hip for lefthanded players).

The Two-handed Backhand Grip

The two-handed backhand grip is nothing new. Players like Viv McGrath in 1938, Pancho Segura in the 1940s, John Bromwich in 1946, and Frew Mc-Millan, Chris Evert and Jimmy Connors in the 1970s, have all won many tournaments using the two-handed backhand. And let us not forget Bjorn Borg, who won Paris and Wimbledon five times. However, the two-handed backhand still comes up for a lot of criticism and there is much dispute over whether it is a good idea to teach it to youngsters. I believe the decision should be totally up to the player. Small children may well want to start with two hands, as it will enable them to manoeuvre the racquet more easily. But later on, if they are ambitious, I believe they should be able to try a one-handed stroke.

How to Get the Two-handed Backhand Grip
The two-handed backhand grip is just like the one-handed backhand grip described above, except that the second hand is wrapped around the raquet in front of the guiding hand for extra support and strength.

Advantages
- You are able to play the ball more in front, with an open stance, and take the ball quicker after the bounce. This could help you especially on the return of service.
- With two hands you can play harder shots as you have twice the strength of the wrist behind the shot.
- The second hand can help you put more topspin on the ball. Because you can apply more explosiveness and speed to the shot, you will be able to give the ball more rotation.
- It will help you to conceal the direction of the shot you are about to play, and its kind. It is difficult for the opponent to see from the way you bring the racquet into the ready position whether you going to play a lob, drive or angled shot. This advantage applies especially to the passing shot (*see p. 50*).
- If you are not that strong, it will help you to spread the muscle tension.

Disadvantages
- The biggest disadvantage of the two-handed backhand is its limited reach, particularly when returning a slice service, which is designed to move away from the body (*see p. 43*).
- It is difficult to apply underspin with the two-handed backhand as the follow through of the left arm is limited.
- It is very limiting when playing low short balls.
- In quick exchanges at the net, trying to change grips from the forehand volley to the two-handed backhand volley can take too long.

GROUNDSTROKES

Position of Player and Racquet

If you are a beginner, I would recommend that your starting position on the court be about 0.5 to 1 metre (1.5 to 3 feet) behind the centre of the baseline, with your face towards the net (oncoming ball, opponent). Your feet should be slightly apart, your knees bent and the upperbody weight on the balls of your feet (*see p. 35*).

Your racquet should be in front of the body, and resting, at the throat, in your nonplaying hand. The playing hand should be lightly gripping the handle with the elbows slightly bent beside the body.

Balance and Footwork

The four most important factors for the groundstroke are:
- Grips
- Balance
- Strokes
- Tactics

We could start with tactics, but if you are not able to master the first three, good tactics will not help you at all.

It may surprise you, but balance is the most important factor. No doubt you have seen professionals at work and don't they make it look easy? Well, there is one fundamental skill that they all have in common: good balance. You may say, 'But they don't hit the ball at all in the way you tell me to.' This is quite true, but it is also why balance is so important. The pace of the top players is very fast and there is often no time to get into the 'correct' positions recommended for the beginner. The better you become, the more you need to improvise. There are occasions when you will have to play on the wrong foot or jump off the ground à la Jimmy Connors or Steffi Graf. These players have spent many years learning the basics, and are therefore able to confidently improvise.

The key to good balance is good footwork. It decides the basis for the balance of the stroke and will help you to execute the stroke better. To achieve good footwork you must make sure that your feet are not planted with the heels on the ground. Keep your weight on the balls of your feet, moving lightly between shots. Knees should be slightly bent, feet a little apart and toes pointed at the net. That way you can shift your bodyweight easily in any direction — a light sportscar can manoeuvre much more quickly than a heavy truck.

Make sure that when you move to the righthand side, you move your right foot first, so that you don't cross over with your left foot. The same thing applies to movement to the lefthand side. Move your left foot first.

A fraction of a second before you are going to hit the ball make sure your feet are planted. While you are stroking the ball your bodyweight should be transferred to the front foot. Immediately after the followthrough of the stroke, resume your original position on the court so as to be ready for the next shot. Never stay still — you should always be slightly on the move. For the top players, the pace has become so fast that most balls are hit on the run. The time needed for a firm hitting stance is simply not there.

The most common mistake the beginner makes is to step too close with the left foot (on the forehand) or with the right foot (on the backhand) to the bounce of the ball. For lefthanded players it is right foot on the forehand and left foot on the backhand.

Always make sure you step forward towards the net and not sideways. The only exception to this rule is the wide ball, when it may be necessary to move sideways to reach it. This is known as a 'close stance'. There is one other possibility, called the 'open stance'. This is when the feet stay in place and a pivot is made with the upperbody. However, this should not be used

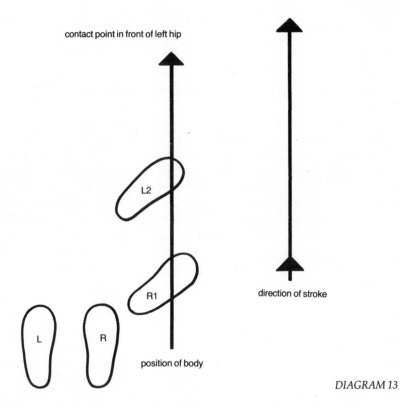

contact point in front of left hip

L2

R1

direction of stroke

L   R

position of body

DIAGRAM 13

Footwork for the forehand for righthanded players. Move the right foot first and during the stroking of the ball transfer bodyweight to the left (front) foot.

by beginners and never on the backhand. When stepping towards the net always remember to turn the shoulder well so that you are looking over it to the oncoming ball.

Hitting the Ball

The Backswing

The most logical motion for the backswing would be straight back, but in practice this is difficult to achieve and most players make a small curve upwards. The rhythm of the swing should be very smooth and relaxed. If you are a beginner do not try too big a backswing. The intermediate player can use a longer backswing (it will give more pace to the ball), but will have to adjust to the game situation. It might happen that there is less time and therefore a shortened swing will be called for. A shorter swing for a ball hit on the run is always advisable. Playing on faster court surfaces will also demand shorter backswings.

Betty Stove demonstrates the ready position for receiving the serve.

Hana Mandlikova hitting a forehand volley.

Hana Mandlikova hitting a backhand.

Hana Mandlikova's classic serving action. Note the height of the ball toss.

The Swing

The movement of the arm and racquet should be smooth throughout and increase gradually in speed. Concentrate on the point of impact in front of the body. From the backswing the racquet will come down slightly to meet the oncoming ball at hip level. The racquethead should be relatively flat (vertical) with the elbow pointed to the ground, and the grip should tighten but not become stiff. The racquethead should have more speed than the arm.

On the forehand the arm will be extended, whereas on the backhand the arm will be stretched after the contact point. Both arms should move at the same time, allowing the shoulders to turn as well.

Contact Point

The contact point should always be in front of the hip nearest the net (left hip for the forehand, right hip for the backhand; vice versa for lefthanded players). On the forehand this point will be slightly further back than it is on the backhand. Make sure that at the moment of impact, which you should try to keep as long as possible, you have the racquet good and tight in your hand. As you make contact with the ball, you should transfer your bodyweight to the front foot. Keep the arm stretched, the elbow pointed to the ground and both shoulders at the same height.

The Followthrough

After having made contact the racquethead should continue in the direct line of the ball just hit. Make sure you stay relaxed and keep your movements smooth. The right shoulder will end up higher than the left or vice versa depending on the stroke played. At the end of the followthrough the racquet should be brought back to the ready position.

Advice on the Forehand

The grip I recommend for the forehand is the Eastern grip, in which the V between forefinger and thumb is placed over the back top edge of the racquet handle (*see p. 29*).

Beginners
- Let your racquet do the work.
- Make sure you prepare early by getting to the right place on the court and into the right stance to take the ball. The better prepared you are the better you will be able to concentrate on the contact point.
- Transfer your bodyweight forward on to the front foot as you make contact with the ball.

Advanced Players
- On a short ball go to the net.
- Take the ball early after the bounce.
- On a wide ball, make the extra step so that you can hit around the ball to steer it back into the court.

Advice on the Backhand

The grip I recommend for the backhand is the Backhand grip in which the V between forefinger and thumb is placed over the front top edge of the racquet handle (*see p. 31*).

Beginners
- Take the racquet back early, with the help of the nonplaying hand.
- Let the racquet do the work.
- Keep the stroke simple and hit flat when you have a good balance.

Advanced Players
- On a short ball go to the net and take the ball early.
- On a deep ball, try to take it early.
- On a wide ball, make the extra step so that you can hit around the ball to steer it back into the court.
- When using the two-handed backhand, hit the ball when it is low.

SPINS

Topspin

Topspin is used frequently by many players. It is produced by the racquet strings brushing up and over the ball. After landing the ball bounces high and travels further. Because you have better control with topspin and the ball drops quickly after clearing the net, it is useful for angled shots cross-court and passing shots.

Underspin

Underspin or backspin is made by brushing under the ball with the racquet. A ball that's hit with underspin will go over the net fairly low and will stay very low after bouncing. It is therefore very good for dropshots.

THE SERVICE

If you have a good service it will help you tremendously. With good technique and if well-played tactically, it can win the point outright for you or set you up for a winning shot.

The difference between the service and other shots is that you have the ball in your hand and you can start the point when you are ready. You don't have to react to an opponent's shot. No matter what kind of service you intend to play, you should always use the same stance so that your opponent can't see what kind of service you are going to hit. Be relaxed, observe your opponent's position, decide where you are going to place the service, take a deep breath and execute. If you fail on your first attempt, don't rush into the second service. Concentrate, relax and breathe deeply. Decide where you are going to place it and execute.

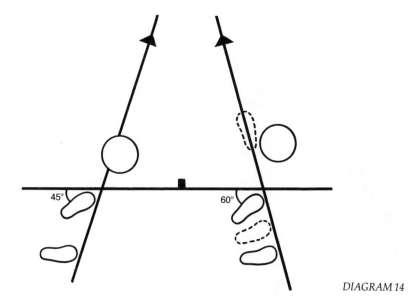

DIAGRAM 14

Position for the serve.

Grip

For the beginner, I recommend the same grip for the service as used for the forehand (*see* Eastern Grip, *p. 29*). The ball will be flat, but you will have good contact with it, and for the beginner that is a good philosophy because your first objective should be to bring the ball into play. It will take you some time to find the right balance and rhythm for the stroke. As you become more advanced you may want to try a grip closer to the Backhand grip. This will enable you to put more spin on the ball.

Position

When serving from the right side of the court make an angle of 60° to the baseline with the left foot. When serving from the left side of the court make an angle of 45° to the baseline with the left foot. Stand about 3–5 centimetres (1–2 inches) behind the line. The right foot should be parallel to the baseline and the feet should be a shoulder's width apart, with the weight placed mainly on the right foot. The shoulders and hips should be side on to the net. A line drawn across the front of the feet towards the net should give the hitting direction. (See Diagram 14.)

With the elbows slightly bent, hold the racquet at chest height and pointed in the hitting direction. Hold the ball in the left hand, palm up, with the fingers slightly bent. Lefthanded players should of course reverse the lefts and rights in these directions.

Toss

To 'toss up', or 'throw up', are the expressions used by many people for this action. To my mind, it should be 'place up', because this is what you do to the ball. You carry the ball up with your left hand high into the air and then hold on to it for as long as possible, as if you were placing it in position ready to be hit. If you let it go a fraction too early it will go to the right; if you let it go a fraction too late it will go to the left. If you throw the ball up in line with the left foot it is possible that the ball will move from front to back. However, it is easier to hit this ball than one which is moving to the left or to the right. If you place the ball too far in front of you it will go into the net. If you place the ball too far behind you it will go out over the serviceline.

The 'placing up' of the ball should last for as long as possible, because that way you will keep your left shoulder and arm well up. If you drop the left arm too soon you will fall away from the shot long before you hit the ball, meaning that you will have no bodyweight behind the shot.

Swinging Movement

At the same time as you release the ball in the toss, the racquethand should start the backward swing. Both arms are now above the shoulder. The ball is released and the racquet starts the 'behind-the-back scratch' motion. Drop the racquethead low and come out accelerating to meet the ball at the highest possible point. Just before the contact point, you should start transferring your bodyweight from the backfoot to the front foot. This shift in weight, along with the acceleration of the racquethead and snap of the wrist at impact, will give you the speed and control necessary for the shot.

Contact Point

If you ever saw Roscoe Tanner toss for the service in his top years, you would know that he played the ball *before* it had reached its highest point. His swing was so fast that he was able to hit the ball on the way up. With Steffi Graf, however, her throw is so high that she hits the ball on the way down. Both players had or have excellent services, so what is the best moment to make contact with the ball?

The best moment to hit the ball, of course, is when it is at its highest point. In other words, as far as you can reach with your racquet. If you can do that time after time, it will mean that you have made contact in the same place in every single service. Make a mental picture of yourself, with your toes right through to the extended racquet arm all in one line. Your arm is stretched, your body is stretched, your legs are stretched and your toes are stretched.

The most difficult thing is to place the ball twice in a row in exactly the same spot. One ball might be so high that you have to jump for it, while another might be so low that you have to hit it beside your ear. Of course these are extremes, but I just wanted to emphasize how difficult it is to throw the ball up the same way every time.

When placing the ball allow a margin of 4–10 centimetres (1.5–4 inches) above your total extension, so that you can let it drop a bit and still hit with full force. Make the contact last as long as possible because this will give you control of the ball. The back foot should move forward towards the front foot and you should be standing on your toes so that you are fully extended right through from the toes to the tip of the racquethand.

Remember, place the ball above and slightly in front of your left foot, and hit it at your maximum extension.

Followthrough

After the contact point you will step into the court, right foot first, and automatically end up with the racquet down on the left side of your body.

Make sure that when you have finished the stroke you don't just stand there admiring the result — the ball may come back quicker than you think. I remember the first time I played baseball and to my surprise and the surprise of others I hit the ball, sending it far, far away. I was so stunned I just kept standing there, looking. My friends finally woke me up, screaming at me that I was supposed to run to first base.

Three Basic Services

The Flat Service

The flat service has no rotation because the ball is hit square on the racquet and it is sometimes played with the forehand or Eastern grip (*see p. 29*). It is a good choice for a first service, or when trying to hit an ace (non-returnable ball), because it can earn you a quick point. However, on the second service, use an option — any of the spin serves — that allows you to have more control, as you do not want to get a double fault.

The Slice Service

For the slice service you use the Backhand grip (*see p. 31*). The motion of the swing is the same except that the ball is tossed a little more to the right. Then with a sharp snap of the wrist, the ball will spin from right to left. The ball bounce will be lower and on faster court surfaces will slide more.

This is a good first service, as it places the ball to the right of the opponent's forehand, drawing play outside the court. It is especially good on slower courts where there is more spin and lower bounce, and also on grass because it gives the opponent no time to get back for the next shot. However, if it is not performed well (not enough spin or not enough height), the ball may be too short and therefore easy to attack.

The Topspin (Kick) Service

For the topspin service, like the slice service, you use the backhand grip, but this time the ball is tossed more to the left and behind your head. The racquethead is moved very fast in a slightly left to right motion.

The topspin serve is a good choice for the second service. The ball goes high over the net, drops quickly into the court and bounces high. It is also good for the serve and volley point, especially when mixed with the slice

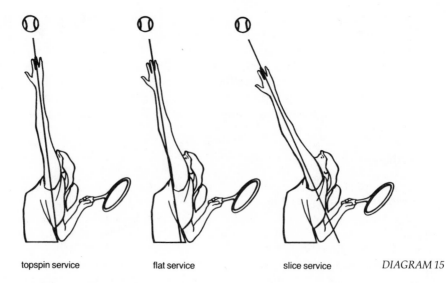

| topspin service | flat service | slice service | *DIAGRAM 15* |

Ball toss for the three types of serve.

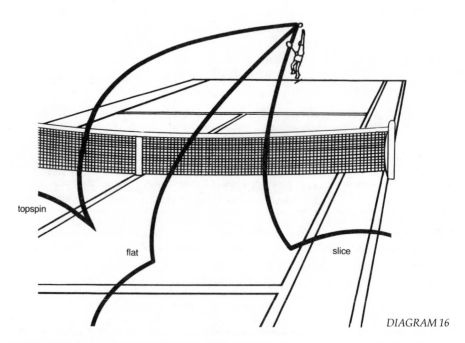

DIAGRAM 16

The direction and bounce of the ball on the three types of serve.

serve. The topspin serve does, however, require a strong back because the ball is tossed to the left which means you have to arch your back to hit it properly.

THE VOLLEY

The volley is a shot played before the ball has bounced. The ball is taken out of the air and placed directly back on the opponent's side of the net. Most volleys are played with underspin (or slice) as this gives the player more control.

Grip

On the forehand volley the forehand or Eastern grip should be used (*see p. 29*) and on the backhand volley the Backhand grip should be used (*see p. 31*). However, if ball exchanges at the net are very fast I would recommend the semi-Continental grip (*see p. 30*).

Ready Position

Your nonplaying hand should hold the racquet at the throat and the playing hand should be relaxed at the grip. The feet should be slightly apart, knees slightly bent, and elbows pointing to the ground.

Swing Motion

Your opponent's passing shot (*see p. 50*) will come fast and you will not have much time for the backswing, so keep it short. You don't need to turn the shoulder far on the volley. Your right hand should only go back as far as your right shoulder, no further because you don't have the time. Your weight should be back and your eyes on the ball. Lefthanded players should of course reverse the lefts and rights in these instructions.

Contact Point

The contact point should be in front of your left shoulder. The stroke should be made with a firm wrist and be crisp, snappy and decisive. The racquet should stop as it meets the ball, with the left arm being used for balance.

General Advice

For the low volley, bend your knees and open your racquet face to lift the ball over the net. Low volleys should be blocked and hit deep while high volleys (waist or head high) can either be blocked or hit at an angle. Very high volleys must be played at speed.

Always remember that a volley is an attacking shot and that it relies more on placement than speed to win. With your proximity to the net you are able to use all your opponent's forecourt, so choose your angles well from that position. However, don't get too close or you will be lobbed. Two of the best volleyers in the game today are Martina Navratilova and John McEnroe.

The Split-Step and Half Volley

The split-step and half volley is a stroke used by top players on the service line, in between giving a service and playing the first volley. Sometimes, when running into the net after the service to play a volley, it is not possible to get there in time, and it is necessary to let the ball bounce. The player is too far advanced to use a groundstroke and the only option is to play a cross between a drive and a volley — a half volley. Directly after the bounce the open racquet face is placed under the ball. The ball is not hit; this is a touch stroke and it requires precise timing and control. With the body bent low and the weight back, the ball is lifted up without bringing the head up. The aim is to place the ball deep in the opponent's court so as to allow time to be ready for the passing shot.

THE SMASH OR OVERHEAD

The smash, also sometimes called the overhead, is not an easy stroke to learn. It can only be played after a lob. As the ball passes high over your head, you have the chance to smash it. The word 'smash' says it all. Smash it. Win it. Finish the point.

When faced with a high ball, try to smash it instead of volleying it. With the smash you have more power and speed and a well-placed smash to an empty corner can win the point outright. Be aware of where your opponent is or is going, and then place the ball where he isn't.

The motion for the smash is basically the same as for the service, the only major difference being in the backswing. On the smash the backswing is much shorter. The ball is hit out of the air while high and out in front or sometimes after a high bounce.

To make the smash you should first turn sideways to the net by moving the right foot back. Lift the racquet up, behind the back (back-scratching), and with your left hand point at the ball. This is not to actually point at the ball but to keep your balance. Then move your feet in small steps, so as to get into position underneath the ball. Let the wrist and hand do the work for you. Keep the wrist firm as you hit the ball. Try to hit the ball just with the arm rather than shoulder it. On the followthrough you don't bring your racquet all the way down as you do in the service.

You should be able to *hit* a smash from anywhere on the court and be able to *place* a smash anywhere on the court. To hit a smash from anywhere you must learn to recognize a lob early and then you will have time to prepare. The key to successful smashing is being ready under the ball in a balanced position. In deciding where to place the ball for a winning shot, you know where the ball came from and where your opponent was last. While you move, watch where your opponent is going. Then decide immediately where you are going to make your shot and don't hesitate. Go for it. Don't always smash the same corner, try to catch your opponent out.

When the ball comes shorter don't think, 'This is easy, I'm going to clobber this ball'. Take your time, get ready early and let the racquet do the work. Don't try to hasten your shot and don't try to overhit.

As I said earlier, you can also use a smash after the ball has bounced. If your opponent plays a deep defensive lob (*see p.48*) it will come over the net so high that you will know it is going to bounce high. In this case you can sometimes let it bounce and then smash it. This will give you more time to see where your opponent is and the timing will be easier. A ball that comes full speed out of the sky on the perpendicular isn't easy to hit, so let it bounce, take your time and play it back with spin to control it better.

As with all strokes, make sure that you shift your weight from the back foot to the front foot. The ideal point of contact is when your racquet is totally stretched out.

One very difficult shot for the beginner and even for the very advanced player is the backhand smash. I would not recommend putting it in your repertoire. There are plenty of tournament players who don't even know it exists. My advice is to move your feet fast so that you can smash the ball normally. That way you won't get off balance and you can put much more power behind the ball. The only person I know who can play this shot with confidence is Claudia Khode. She learned to play it because she was never fast enough to move under the ball for a normal smash and after years of practice she has it pretty well under control. If you do play it the most important thing is to turn your back to the net so that you have a good free shoulder to hit the ball. Then the snap of the wrist will play the shot for you, but watch the position of the racquethead, and good luck.

THE LOB

In the last section we discussed the smash, but the smash can only be played after a lob. A lob is a high ball that travels through the air right over the opponent's head. There are two kinds of lob, the defensive lob and the offensive lob.

Defensive Lob

A defensive lob is a high ball played to get you out of trouble, such as when you are on the run. Put the ball high in the air over the opponent's head. It will give you time to get back into position to return the next shot. Most players don't really practise this shot, but take my advice: take time to learn it because it can earn you a lot of points. I know there is more satisfaction in playing a hard passing shot or a strong drive right down the line, but when it comes to points the lob has the same value as any other shot. If the net player is expecting a passing shot the lob can take him completely by surprise.

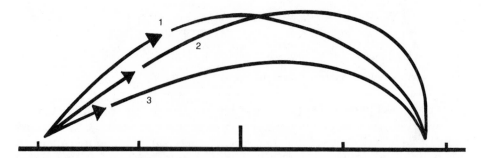

DIAGRAM 17

Height of the ball over the net on the three types of serve.
1. Defensive
2. Offensive topspin
3. Offensive slice

Forehand Defensive Lob

The grip for the forehand lob is the same as that used for the forehand, the Eastern grip (*see p. 29*). You will have to get under the ball more and guide it away over the opponent's serviceline. Many defensive lobs have to be hit in the open stance (*see p. 33*) and also on the run. To control the shot you will need to follow through well. If the ball simply bounces off the strings it could land anywhere. Make sure you feel the ball well on the strings. Get right under it with an open racquet face for this feel and control. If you aim for height and depth you will be successful.

Backhand Defensive Lob

For the backhand defensive lob use the same grip as you use for your backhand. As before, make sure you get well under the ball and follow it right through.

Offensive Lob

As you can see in the illustration above, the trajectory of the offensive lob is quite different to that of the defensive lob. The defensive lob can be slow, because its main aim is to get you out of trouble. With the offensive lob, however, you have to attack and therefore you have to hit harder. The available space in which to place the ball is rather small. So to aim accurately, aggressively and with control, you have to put a lot of spin on the ball.

Forehand Offensive and Topspin Lob

If you watch the top players in action, you will notice that Mats Willander has an excellent offensive topspin lob. He plays with a Western forehand grip anyway, so it is natural for him to play the topspin lob and that way he can keep his opponent guessing and often catch him on the wrong foot.

For a topspin lob, try to get your grip as close to the Western grip as possible. With this grip you have to hit the ball beside you, instead of out in front. This means you can get right over the ball, which is difficult to do if the ball is too far out in front. So come up and over the ball, letting your racquethead accelerate: the faster your racquet moves over the ball the more rotation you will get. The topspin will quickly bring the ball down.

Backhand Offensive Lob

One of the best offensive backhand lobs in the game today would be Chris Evert's. For a start, her timing is perfect. The moment she usually chooses is just when her opponent has taken that extra step forward to the net. Furthermore, she adds no frills to the shot. By that I mean that the shot is practically flat and she takes the same backswing as she normally does for the groundstroke. She simply takes an overview of the game situation and does what is most efficient to win the point.

Mats Willander uses the topspin backhand for the backhand offensive lob but both players use a two-handed backhand grip which enables them to easily disguise the normal backhand, the backhand passing shot and the backhand lob and so keep their opponents guessing.

The underspin or offensive slice lob with the lower trajectory, shown on Diagram 17, is used by most one-handed players. The spin keeps the ball in, but again, the skill lies in the placement, and timing of the shot. The opponent will be leaning forward and expecting a passing shot. Play the shot quickly and aggressively.

Tactics for Lobbing

For the beginner, the best place to lob is over the opponent's backhand. But once you become a better player, you will also have to learn to lob over your opponent's forehand. It is important to always keep your opponent guessing. Learn to play the lob crosscourt on the longest trajectory and down the line. Never limit your possibilities.

Occasionally you see a lob used during a baseline rally. This is done to change the pace. The opponent will be surprised and thrown off balance. If a player uses it often, as Tracy Austin used to do, you (the opponent) must learn to take the ball out of the air and put it in the angles of the court. As happened to Tracy Austin, the lobber, thinking they have created more time, will be caught off guard.

Practise your lobbing with someone who wants to practise smashing. Or you could just take a bucket of balls and practise on your own. Bounce each ball once, then find the right trajectory for your shot.

THE SLICE

A slice is hit with a fairly open racquethead which goes down and underneath the ball. A slice backhand return will take pace off the ball, especially against a big server. If you block the ball, you will only give it more speed.

By putting slice on the ball you can play it back to the server's feet.

A slice on a defensive shot can get you out of trouble by giving you time to recover from a bad position. A slice will also change the speed of the ball and therefore your opponent's rhythm.

By slicing a shot as you approach the net, you will be able to control it better and make a better placement so that your next shot, a volley at the net, will be easier. Also, the ball will float longer in the air giving you more time to take a better position at the net. Make sure that the ball stays low and your opponent has to lift the ball.

A slice on the volley will produce a winner on fast court surfaces. The opponent will have great difficulty getting under the ball to lift it for a passing shot. And if he does manage to play the ball back, you will have a good net position and great balance for playing the next volley.

THE PASSING SHOT

Passing shots should be hit with topspin for greater control. The best passing shot is hit straight down the line, low over the net and hit hard. If you do this successfully several times your opponent will begin to expect it so you will have to try some other shots, may be short crosscourt passes or some lobs. You must always remember that the main objective is to out-manoeuvre your opponent.

CROSSCOURT SHOTS

Crosscourt shots are most often used in long rallies. Because the court is longer diagonally there is less margin for error. At the beginning of a match it is important to get the right rhythm for your return of service. The best way to do this is by playing crosscourt shots. Once you have settled into your rhythm you can play more aggressively with passing shots.

THE DROPSHOT

The dropshot should be a winning point. If it is played at exactly the right moment in the rally it will be.

The dropshot is a shot with a lot of feel to it. It travels low over the net and bounces as short as possible on the other side. If you are able to give the ball underspin it will be even better because this will make the ball stand up and also give it a little forward movement. Your opponent will have to run hard to the ball and if he does reach it in time the chances are his return will be weak. He has to hit up and over the net from a very close position to the net. Be ready and in position to receive the next shot. You should be able to play a winning passing shot or lob.

The best time to hit a dropshot is when you are standing inside the baseline and your opponent is standing behind the baseline. You have to wait for a shorter ball which bounces around the serviceline. If you play the ball from behind the baseline it becomes a much more difficult shot. The ball would come from much further away and travel more slowly over the net. Your opponent would then have time to get to the ball and hit it back more effectively.

When you hit a dropshot you should disguise it so that your opponent has no clue that it is coming. If he sees what you are going to do he can start sprinting and the surprise element is gone. The best way to prepare for the dropshot is as you would for a groundstroke or approach shot. Take the racquet back as if you were going to play a slice forehand or backhand, that is, a little higher than you would for a flat stroke so that you can put spin on the ball. Then at the last moment, just before you make contact, slow things down to take the pace of the ball. Keep a firm wrist and move towards the ball as if it were a groundstroke. Remember that if the surprise element works the point is already half won. Keep the ball on the strings for as long as possible. Stay in control of it all the time. It is better to hit the ball a little harder than to hit into the net. Even when it is too long your opponent still has to get to it to return it.

The followthrough should be longer than it is with the volley, but not so long as with the groundstroke. The racquethead should follow in the direction that you are aiming the ball and keep moving a little longer after you have hit it. This will give you better control of the ball.

After you have hit this perfect dropshot you should quickly regain your position ready for the next shot. You played the dropshot from no-man's-land (the court space between the baseline and the serviceline), so now move backwards a little to in front of the baseline and see what your opponent is going to do. Be ready for the weak reply. You should now be in a good position to hit a passing shot or lob. Don't move into the net as your opponent will then very likely lob you and you will be worse off. Moving a couple of steps backwards is a much safer option. And be ready for a dropshot reply!

THE APPROACH SHOT

The approach shot is the shot you should use to get yourself to the net. There are many different times when you can go to the net. Immediately after a service or a service return, after an offensive lob, during a rally when you have manoeuvred your opponent out of court, or after your opponent has hit a short ball.

Here I would like to discuss the approach shot made after a short ball from your opponent. The approach shot is the shot hit in between playing a groundstroke and a volley. If you want to play total tennis, you should be able to play the approach shot from both the forehand side and the backhand side. However, even some top players are only able to make the approach shot from the backhand side. You then know that so long as you play on

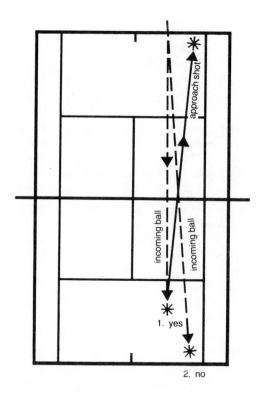

DIAGRAM 18

The approach shot. In the case of '2' the ball was not short enough to make a good approach shot.

their forehand, they will never come to the net whether it be in a rally or after a return of service.

To play the approach shot you have to wait for a shorter ball, and in my mind any ball that lands 2 metres (6.5 feet) in front of the baseline is still a groundstroke. The ball has to be really short to give a good chance of setting the point up for a winner. On fast courts 35 per cent of winners are scored at the net.

When you get that short ball, shorten your backswing, lean into the shot and hit with a firm wrist and arm. The hand and arm should help pull you through the contact zone instead of just the racquethead on its own. This will keep the ball on the racquethead a fraction of a second longer. The 'pause' when you hit the ball should not break your forward momentum. Hit with a full followthrough; the racquethead should follow the intended line of flight of the ball. For more control use underspin. This will make the ball go a little slower through the air giving you time to get a better net position. It will also stay lower after the bounce. You should play the ball down the line so as to give yourself the best chance of a return suitable to volley.

After the shot make sure you end up on the front foot so that you are ready to run for the split-step and the net position. Keep moving forward but not to the middle of the court: move to the middle of all possible returns.

The key to a successful approach shot is recognizing which is the shorter ball to come in on. When you have hit a million balls you will know instinctively which is the right one. If you are very quick compared to your opponent you may be able to get away with a less than perfect approach shot. Of course when you know that your opponent has a particular weakness you will always play your approach shot with that in mind so as to draw an easy volley. And if you know that your opponent tends to play back everything high and slow, you should approach as often as possible.

Jimmy Connors uses the approach shot extremely well. With five or six groundstrokes he'll manoeuvre his opponent into a position outside the court from where he knows he will not receive an offensive shot. Then after a good approach shot Jimmy will usually get a shoulder high volley which he can place for a winner.

John McEnroe uses many variations of the approach shot. Sometimes he comes in with a topspin approach and sometimes with a floating deep ball. John has a very quick eye and is extremely quick at the net in finishing the point. Martina Navratilova also has a good approach shot although she does have the tendency to jump a little on the shot.

To get a really good safe approach shot you will need to hit many balls. Keep at it because you will eventually get the hang of it. You may find on some surfaces, such as clay, that your footing is not as firm and also that the ball bounces more slowly. You will then have to wait for exactly the right shot to make your move to the net. Be smart and alert enough to play the right kind of game for the surface and the opponent.

BASIC TACTICS

It is easy to say that if you do this or that you will win the point. But easy it is not.

Let's start at the beginning. The most important winning tactic the beginner should keep in mind is to be consistent. I have watched many matches played by beginners (they are actually great fun) where the greatest achievement of the players was simply being able to keep the ball in play. Sometimes the ball would go over the net at 2 metres (6.5 feet), sometimes it would go over at 10 metres (33 feet). Every time the ball bounced, they had to let it come down to waist level before returning it and this meant a lot of moving to get into the right position. However, These players understood very well that simply by sheer consistency they might win the match.

There are of course a lot of other important points to remember. For the beginner most shots should be deep crosscourt with an occasional forehand down the line. If you practise that right from the beginning you will have a good winning base. And always remember height. If you hit the ball too high it could go out, and if you hit it too low it could go into the net. Make sure that every time you are drawn out of court you come straight back to the beginning position. That is, the spot in the middle of the court about 50 centimetres to 1 metre (1.5 to 3 feet) behind the baseline. And make sure you you always control the stroke. It is easy to hit hard but if you cannot control the ball the shot will be useless. Power in the stroke comes from the speed of your swing and from the transference of your weight. The stroke should be easy, smooth, well-coordinated and relaxed. You will then have control.

As you improve, you should try to do more than simply put the ball back into the opponent's court. This is when depth becomes important. By depth I mean how far down the opponent's court the ball bounces. Even for the top player depth is important, because it keeps the opponent on the defence. A flat stroke with an easy swing and a little more height over the net will give you the depth you want. You are now in a position to start directing the ball to the opponent's forehand or backhand, or down the middle of the court. Find out your opponent's weak side, it is usually the backhand, and direct the ball to that side. Try to make the ball bounce about 1.5 metres (5 feet) from the baseline. Hit the ball out to the corners and keep hitting to the backhand, especially when you yourself are in trouble. It will open up the rest of the court and with a good crosscourt forehand you might win the point. If you are in trouble on a wide forehand play it safe and hit the ball back crosscourt. Give yourself time to get back into the point.

As you improve you should also start thinking about placing your service. Try to hit the first service to your opponent's backhand. At this stage don't do anything special with the second service, just get it *in*. But later you could place both the first and second service to the backhand. By this time you should have a good feeling of control on the service.

When you are beginning to feel quite confident and in control of your game, you should start using the approach shot and playing at the net. Wait for a shorter ball and play the shot to your opponent's weakness. You should also be making use of the passing shot and lob when your opponent is at the net. Learn all these shots well and when to use them.

Roger Gould

Hana Mandlikova hitting a forehand.

Martina Navratilova's backswing in preparation for the backhand.

For the forehand lob, hit under the ball and guide it over the opponent's serviceline.

To control the lob properly, you must follow through well.

PLAYING SINGLES

STARTING THE GAME

Now that you have studied all the basic shots in tennis, we need to talk about the whole game. Let's pretend that we are starting a game. The first thing to do is decide who will serve first. This is usually done by a spin of the racquet. Well, sorry, but I have won the spin and I now have one of four choices:

1. I can choose to serve.
2. I can choose to receive.
3. I can choose which side of the net to start on.
4. I can give the choice to you.

If I decide to serve and I win the first game, I will have the psychological advantage of being ahead every time we change ends. You, on the other hand, will have to win a game every time just to make the score even. This burden will place extra pressure on you.

If I decide to receive and give the first service turn to you, you may not be totally warmed up. I might have a good chance to break your service which would give me a good edge. On top of that I will have another game to warm up in before I have to serve myself. Also, every time I serve we will have just changed ends, meaning that I will have had time to sit down, dry my hands and generally pep myself up for the next game.

Suppose you won the toss and have decided to serve. That leaves me with the choice of sides. The relevant factors here are the wind and sun. Do I like to play with the wind or against it? Which end will put the sun in my eyes? In fact these factors shouldn't really bother me. One time or another I will have to serve against the wind or the sun or whatever.

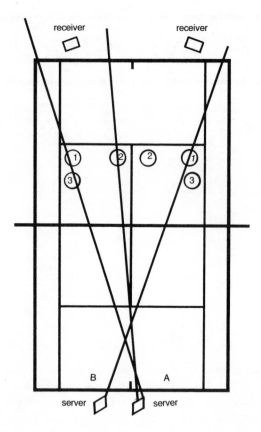

DIAGRAM 19

The three best placements for the first service from 'A' the deuce-court and 'B' the ad-court. The best placement is marked '1'.

THE SERVICE

The service is a major stroke in today's tennis. It can set up the point for you right away by putting you in the driver's seat and forcing a weak return.

Of course the male top player will always score more points with the service than the female. He can serve faster and the receiver will have less time to make his return. And even if he manages to make it he may not have enough time to do something threatening with it. On the faster courts particularly, the men can really take advantage and pound the serve away. Of course it helps a lot if you have a powerful service. Boris Becker won Wimbledon twice with his great service, although on slower surfaces he has not done so well. The reason for this is that on slower courts, although the

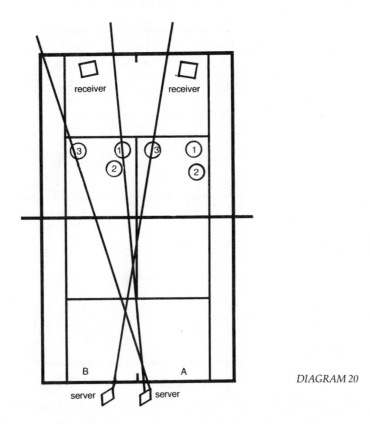

DIAGRAM 20

The three best placements for the second service from 'A' the deuce-court and 'B' the ad-court. The best placement is marked '1'.

server's speed stays the same, the rougher court surface slows up the bounce and height of the ball. This gives the receiver a little more time to cover the court and stand in closer to cut down the angle of the spin. He can take the ball more quickly and play it back smoothly to the server. So the mighty service of the faster court is diminished to a normal service. It is then up to such players to prove that their other strokes are dependable.

Position of Server and Receiver

As a singles player you have to defend your side of the court alone so it is advisable not to stand too far away from the middle of the court. In any case you are never allowed to serve beyond the singles sideline. Your feet are not allowed to touch anything inside the court. The court also means the lines. Even if it is only by 1 millimetre or a fraction of an inch you have still

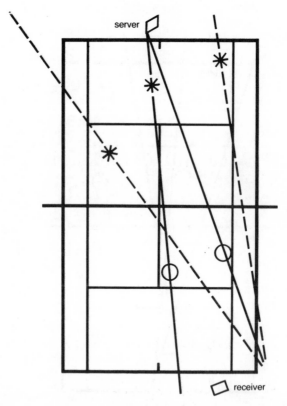

server

receiver

DIAGRAM 21

The position of the receiver. The solid line shows the serve down the middle and the direction of the backhand return along the same path. A serve out wide to the forehand allows the receiver to return down the line or crosscourt.

touched the line. Don't take the risk. Stand at least 3 centimetres (1 inch) away from the baseline. You might turn one foot slightly and make a footfault without knowing it. Remember, good practice makes good habits.

As the receiver you should put yourself in a straight line across from the server over the servicecourt. Stand so that you have an equal opportunity to return on both the forehand and backhand side. You should be on the balls of your feet, knees slightly bent, arms in front, and able to move in any direction. Concentrate. Watch the server. Watch his movements. The faster the ball comes the quicker you will have to react. Watch the ball go up in the air. Try to see where the server is going to hit. Anticipate quickly. Try to take the ball early so as to give less time to the server to prepare for the next shot.

Placing the Ball

In the beginning the most important thing is just to get the ball into the servicecourt. Later, as you improve and get more control, you should place

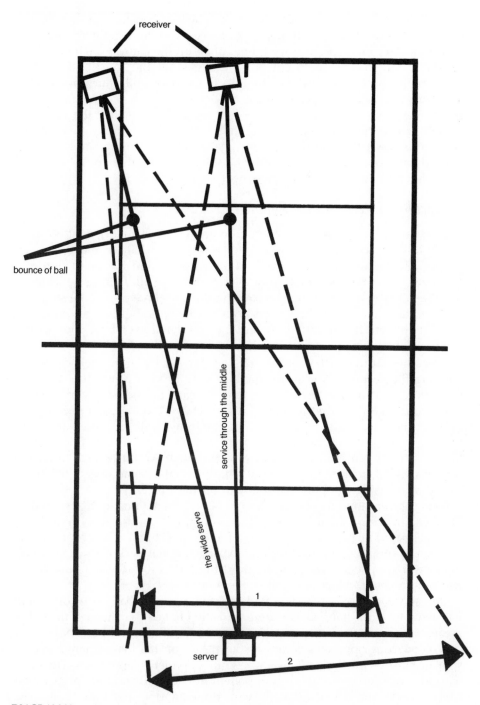

DIAGRAM 22

Return of service. The area marked '1' must be defended after serving through the middle. The wider area marked '2' has to be defended after serving wide.

the ball on your opponent's backhand. You should constantly be gaining in speed and control. The next step is to serve everything right through the middle of the court. That way you don't open up the court. Watch how your opponent returns. Learn to cut out the angles on the court and learn to make angles on the court depending on the surface and your opponent.

In Diagram 22 showing the returns of service, you can see that when you serve wide you give your opponent two distinct choices for the return: a straight down the line return or a short-angled crosscourt return. When you serve down the middle, however, your opponent hasn't much choice other than to put the ball back in the middle, meaning that you, the server, won't have to move much for your next shot.

General Advice on the Service

The service is one occasion when you do get a second chance so it is worth taking a little more risk with the first service. Hit it harder and flatter. Or deeper and wider. This will give you a chance to win the point outright. However, don't fall into the trap of overhitting the ball. During my clinics I have seen many brave young men overhit the ball. I have seen the smiles of pride on their faces. 'See how hard I can hit the ball.' But the percentage of serves that went in was very low, and they were followed by a poor second service. Remember, power means nothing without control.

It has been proven that evenly ranked players have an even chance of winning the second service. So, the best way to start a match is to put a little more spin on the first service and increase the odds in your favour. Once you have your rhythm and confidence you can also add speed.

Don't start rushing, keep doing the same thing, only play the ball a little harder. Your personal percentage of first services in should not change. Mine is 65 per cent and I am happy with that. It would be nice to have a higher percentage but then I would have to take some speed off and I would start losing the points I now win on the first service.

Some players love to play a game of serve, then into the net to volley. They use their opponent as a target, ensuring that almost every return will be a volley good for them by using spin to give them more control. The returner is simply concentrating on blocking the ball back. In this situation the slower spin serve will give the most trouble to the returner because he will not be able to block the ball.

One service to try is the slow wide spinning service ball. Your opponent will have to work hard to get there and the chance that he will miss it is greater. A deep soft service to the backhand is another good play. No matter how good your opponent is, always keep him on his toes. Change speed, spin or slice to put him off balance. Your opponent should have to work hard to earn every point. If your opponent moves badly and his preparation is slow, serve directly at his body with three-quarter speed and spin. The chance that you will get an easy volley on the return is greater. Find out what works well for you and never change a winning game.

In the modern game of tennis there are two basic positions from which you can win points: the baseline and the net. So after you have served make sure that you take one of those positions as quickly as possible. If you hit a very hard service and decide to follow it up to the net, you may become trapped in 'no-man's-land', the court space between the baseline and the serviceline. From there you will have to hit a volley to an opening in the court that is far enough away from the receiver to give you time to move closer to the net for the next shot.

There are two things you should always keep in mind when serving. First, you don't want to lose the attack — to give the initiative to your opponent. This means that you must get your first service in as often as you can. If you do get it in there is a two to one chance that you will win the point. So don't always go for the big boomer, play it safe and use three-quarter speed. Second, always hit the service deep. If you hit it deep it is much more difficult for the receiver to take over the attack, and the odds that you will win your service are increased by 50 per cent. A shallow service, on the other hand, makes your chances of winning even with those of your opponent. So keep it deep.

COURT POSITIONS FOR THE RETURN

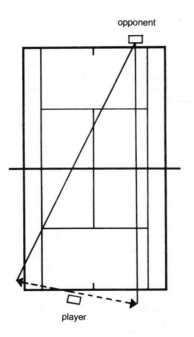

DIAGRAM 23

When you have drawn your opponent wide to the backhand side you should wait for the return shot on the left side of the centre mark. By positioning yourself there you are standing at the centre of all possible returns and you will have to take the same number of steps to the forehand down the line as to the backhand crosscourt.

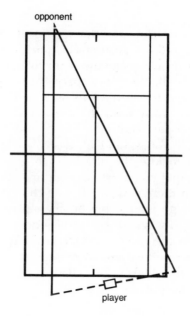

DIAGRAM 24

When you have drawn your opponent wide to the forehand side you should wait for the return shot on the right side of the centre mark. By positioning yourself there you are standing at the centre of all possible returns and you will have to take the same number of steps to the forehand as to the backhand.

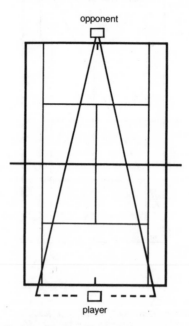

DIAGRAM 25

When you have played a ball through the middle of the court, you should wait for the return shot at the exact centre of the court. The distance to either forehand or backhand is then the same.

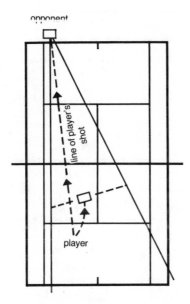

When you go to the net after an approach shot you should wait for the return shot at the centre of all possible returns. The distance for either forehand volley or backhand volley is then the same. With regard to depth you should stand halfway between the net and serviceline.

TYPES OF PLAY IN SINGLES AND GENERAL TACTICS

Baseline Play

After serving a baseline player will normally return to a position behind the baseline, close to the centre mark so that he can move quickly to either side. A good opponent will then alternate well from the forehand to the backhand corner, to keep the baseliner on the run (see shots 1 and 2 on Diagram 27). Hitting on the run is more difficult and the baseliner may well start making mistakes. If the baseliner is too strong the opponent may pull him to the net with a shorter ball (see shot 3 on Diagram 27). After taking shot 3 the baseliner has to decide whether to go quickly to the net for a volley or retreat behind the baseline again. Going back to the baseline without losing your balance for the next stroke is very difficult. It is much better to be aggressive and take the net. The pressure is then put back on the opponent to try a passing shot or a lob.

Net Play

If you have gone to the net don't be timid. Make your shots confident and always move forward for the volley. Your chances at the net to win the point are much greater.

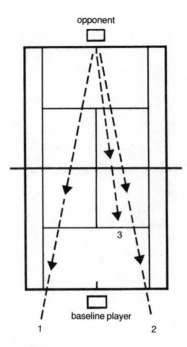

DIAGRAM 27

Shots to the baseline player.
1. *Shot to the backhand corner.*
2. *Shot to the forehand corner.*
3. *Shorter ball to pull the baseline player to the net.*

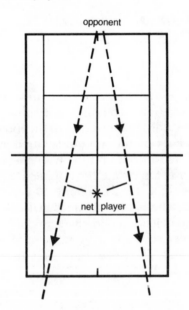

DIAGRAM 28

Position of the net player in the centre of the court, halfway between net and serviceline.

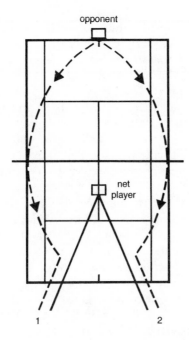

DIAGRAM 29

Lobs used to beat the net player.
1. Lob over the backhand side.
2. Lob over the forehand side.

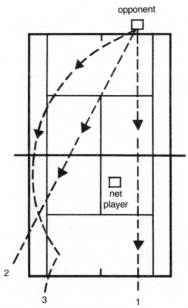

DIAGRAM 30

Tactics used to beat a net player.
1. Down the line passing shot.
2. Short angled passing shot.
3. Lob over the backhand side.

The net player should position himself in the centre of the court halfway between the net and the serviceline. Never stand *too* close to the net or you will make yourself vulnerable to lobs. If you do go right in close, come back a little and be ready for the next shot.

Usually you need to play two volleys before you can win a point at the net. The first volley is played from further back and you will have to hit it deep. The second and hopefully winning volley should be played from a position very close to the net as this will enable you to angle it well. If you watch the top net players you will see that they usually try to control the game from close to the net, especially on the faster courts where the ball doesn't bounce that high.

The opponent can try to beat the net player in several ways. The most common tactic is the passing shot. Mats Willander favours a backhand passing shot which goes down the line but be careful. If you are expecting a down the line shot and move a fraction too soon in that direction, the opponent may use an angled crosscourt shot or lob instead. So be ready to move in any direction, even if you are not playing Mats.

The other shot that is very effective against the net player is the lob. If the net player cannot smash the ball he will have to go all the way back to the baseline to get it. He has then lost his net position and his initiative. Keep lobbing even if the net player is getting them all back. He must eventually tire and start missing.

If the net rusher comes in after a crosscourt approach shot, try to pass him down the line. And make sure you close in after you have hit the ball. The net player's volley is likely to be a weak one and by closing in you are in perfect position to make a winner. An angled passing shot can be softer but one down the line should be hit hard. For your passing shot you can use topspin or slice. Topspin will make the volley more difficult for the net player and the ball will often jump up to give you an easier shot. If you use slice, the net player will have to really open up his raquet face or the ball will go into the net. Whatever, make sure the net player has to *earn* his point.

When playing against a net player the baseline player must stay cool and conceal his intentions. If you are going to play a passing shot or a lob, hold on and disguise the shot until the last moment. Always keep the net rusher guessing.

Total Tennis

In my mind this is the best kind of game to play. A total tennis player can combine all kinds of approaches and can choose the tactics for every single point. The long-term objective should be to be able to play an excellent game of tennis against any type of player and on any kind of surface.

The total tennis player has a very good baseline game and on the first short ball will follow up to the net for a winning volley. They can mix attack and defence, net play and smashes. That way they are not having to rely solely on their passing shot or volley.

The total tennis player builds his game according to the style of the opponent. Compare matches between Chris Evert and Martina Navratilova, the baseline player and the net rusher, with matches between Steffi Graf and Martina Navratilova, the total player and the net rusher. The net rusher may beat the baseliner, but the total player comes out on top.

Play to your opponent's weaknesses but make good use of your strong shots too. For example, instead of playing all shots to your opponent's weaker backhand, play to it only on the important key points. Three-quarters of the points you win in tennis are due to errors on the part of the opponent while only a quarter are made by winning shots. Play percentage tennis. This means choosing the shot that is most effective with the least risk.

To play percentage tennis you have to hit the ball at a certain height over the net. For baseline play it is 1 metre (3 feet), otherwise the ball will not have enough depth. It is possible to hit deep, hard and low over the net, all at the same time, but it is much more risky. The return of service, hard passing shots, dropshots, short angled shots and flat services should go over at 30 centimetres (1 foot), not less. Normal rally balls, approach shots, angled shots and topspin services should go over somewhere between 60 centimetres (2 feet) and 1 metre (3 feet). Anything over 3.5 metres (11.5 feet) is good for a lob.

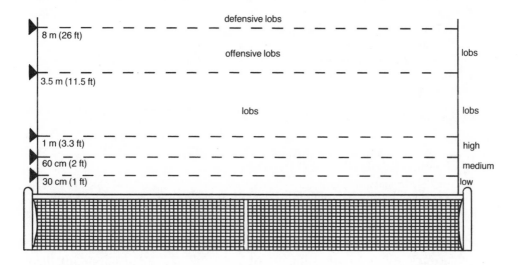

DIAGRAM 31

Height of the ball over the net.
30 cm (1 ft): return of service when server comes in; flat service; passing shots; dropshots; short crosscourt drives.
60 cm (2 ft): return of service when server stays back; forehand; backhand; approach shot; short crosscourt passing shots.
1 m (3.3 ft): high balls to get position back.

General Tactics

In tennis there are two main ways to win points. The first is to place the ball so that the opponent can't play it back or so that he is forced to make an error, for example, play off the wrong foot. The second is to create a situation, usually at the net, in which you can play an outright winner.

Playing somebody for the first time can be difficult as you don't know his or her game. On the circuit you will see many upsets when a new and talented player joins. But after a while, as the other players study the newcomer, there are no more surprises. Scouting a newcomer is important and with the help of your coach you can work out a strategy to follow. Many of the top players keep books and matchnotes on other players.

Make sure you work out a strategy that you can play. There is no sense in deciding to play high topspin to the opponent's backhand if you don't normally use topspin. Likewise, a plan with twist services won't help you much if twist services are not in your repertoire. And if you can only play from the baseline, play from the baseline. Play your strongest shot to your opponent's weakest shot. Place the ball where your opponent isn't. Find a style that suits you and work out your game plan accordingly.

Here are seven basic points to always keep in mind:

1. Play CONSISTENTLY. This should become automatic.
2. DICTATE the way the point is played. This gives you control of the game.
3. VARY your shots and pace. This can upset the tempo of your opponent and make him lose confidence.
4. Play PERCENTAGE tennis and keep a GAME PLAN.
5. Be PATIENT and CONCENTRATE.
6. THINK a stroke AHEAD.
7. FIGHT TILL THE END.

And remember: *The most important stroke is the next stroke.*

KEY SCORES IN SINGLES

In an earlier chapter I explained the scoring system but now I would like to tell you something about the value of the points. The score is a record not only of points won or lost, but it also dictates, combined with your playing style, the type of shot you should play next.

Of course every point is important but some are more important than others. To take two extremes: Having won the first set you are now up five games to four and the current game score is 30–15 in your favour. The next two points can decide the outcome of the match for you. By contrast, if you are in the first set of a match and the score is two games all, the following point is important but it will not weigh as much as matchpoint. But there are many key points in a match. Let's look at it more closely.

Imagine you are the server. The score is 0–0 and you want to make a firm start with the game. Let your intentions be known and apply some intimidation techniques. The receiver will also try to take the initiative. Even if he loses the first game he should still make sure that you, the server, have cause to worry somewhat. This first point can set the mood of the whole game.

At 15−0 you have a chance to get ahead by two points, to 30−0. The receiver, on the other hand, has to play this shot safe just to make the score even at 15−all. At 0−15 you, as server, are under pressure to win the next point because you don't want to be down two points against your serve. You need to use a good safe service, that is, at the same time, deep and attacking, otherwise the receiver will put too much pressure on and you will be in the defensive position. If you lose that point the score will be 0−30 and you then have to win four points to win the game; while your opponent only has to win two points to win the game or one point to get to 40−all (deuce). For the receiver at 0−15 it is well worth a bit of a gamble for a 0−30 lead. Even if he or she doesn't win the point the score will still be even at 15−all.

15−all is an important point in the game. It gives both server and receiver a chance to jump in the game to 30−15 or 15−30, and these scores are both crucial. At 15−all both server and receiver should play for the highest percentage − the most effective shot with the least risk. You, the server, have a slight advantage because you start the point with your service and can decide what kind of point you want to play. If you win the point the score will be 30−15 and for you this is now the key point in the game. If you win the next point the score will be 40−15, and an excellent base from which to win the game because the receiver would have to win at least four points, two of those in a row, before he could win. If, on the other hand, from 15−all the score goes to 15−30, you, the server, will have to play very basic tennis. If you lose the next point you will have to win at least four points, two of those in a row, to win the game. For the receiver, at 15−40 the chances of winning the game are very good. When Steffi Graf reaches this stage she loves to run around her backhand trying to win the point with a forehand shot.

At 30−all and deuce, you, as server, should keep to basics. You should serve so that you get an easier volley. Keep the receiver on his toes by changing your placement of the service. At this stage the receiver should be the hungry wolf, ready to attack, only two points away from winning the game. Good concentration and good hustling are worth a lot.

At 40−30 you, the server, should be serving hard. A high topspin serve to the backhand is a good idea. The receiver should attack in such a way that the server is under pressure to make an error. This is one of the points that Chris Evert, as receiver, plays so well. If you look at her matches you will see that overall, she is not the attacking player, but on 40−30 she will come to the net and try to force an error out of the opponent.

If the score has reached 30−40, you, the server, have obviously already made some mistakes. You should serve solidly while the receiver should run around, especially on a short second service, and attack with his strongest stroke. In the case of advantage server or advantage receiver the respective players should apply the same instructions as given for 40−30 and 30−40.

Another possibility is 0−40 or 40−0. At 0−40 you, the server, have to win five points in a row to win the game. You should play good aggressive tennis. If you hold back the receiver will take the attack (at least he should). The receiver can afford to gamble because he has more points to take a risk with. If you win a point it can put a damper on the receiver. You win not only the point but you also gain some ground psychologically. At 40−0, on the other hand, the receiver has nothing to lose and might as well really go for it. If he or she wins a point it could in turn have a dampening effect on you, the server.

The seventh game in a set is the most important. Try your hardest for this game. Whether the score is 5−1, 4−2 or 3−3 the seventh game is the *big* game in the set. So speed up the pace a little with extra spin and more aggression. Go all out as server or receiver. At 3−3 I prefer to serve, knowing that if I win the game I could break for 5−3 and serve for the set. If I am receiving at 3−3 I also want to win the next game knowing that I then only have to hold my serve to win the set.

Stay cool on matchpoints or setpoints. The last ball has not been decided yet. Keep doing what you were doing before but don't make mistakes.

These are some basic descriptions of game points. Of course an unexpected turn of events can give you a big psychological boost as well as the point. Never change a winning game. Keep doing what you were doing before. And don't be happy with what you have achieved. Always strive for better.

WEATHER CONDITIONS

Playing in the Wind

I am sure you have heard the excuse, 'The wind really bothered me,' given by a player who has just lost. I am always surprised by such an excuse. The opponent had no trouble with the wind. The truth is that the winner was the better player and handled the wind better.

So how do you handle the wind? First of all, you have to follow the ball better with your eyes. Keep light on your feet in case there are unexpected wind changes which move the ball around. To minimize the movement of the ball when serving, toss it a little lower than usual. And hit the first service in, you already have enough problems without adding to them.

When you are playing against the wind you should shorten your back-swing and prepare early for the shot. When you are playing with the wind get to the net as often as you can, nice and close. It is very difficult for the opponent to play a passing shot against the wind. To play a dropshot or a lob when the wind is at your back is not a bright idea. The dropshot will be longer and thus have lost its effectiveness. The lob will be carried by the wind and float away. However, if you play against the wind the dropshot can be very effective. Hit hard against the wind.

Wind can come from all sides. In a side wind don't place the ball near the

When hitting a backhand lob use the same grip as for the backhand drive.

Hit the backhand lob under the ball and guide it under the net as in the forehand lob.

The action for a smash is like that of the serve. You should turn sideways to the net.

After turning sideways for a smash, move under the ball and make sure that your balance is right.

lines. The wind could easily carry the ball 1 metre (3 feet) in one direction or the other.

Always remember that the wind blows as hard for your opponent as it does for you. Put extra effort into the games when you are with the wind. They are the most difficult because you can't hit through the ball. Be smart and concentrate. Look at the flags (if there are any) because the wind sometimes changes during a match.

Playing with the Sun in Your Eyes

The sun may shine on the whole court but it usually gets in the eyes of only one player, and due to the rules of tennis you only have to play at that end for two games in a row before changing with your opponent. Don't get upset about it. Getting upset will only make it worse and waste your energy.

If the sun is shining straight into your eyes during the service, try to move the toss around slightly. Toss a couple of times without hitting to make sure you can see the ball clearly. If you can't see it and nothing else works, hit the ball like a groundstroke. It may look embarrassing but it could give you a better start to the point. Learn to concentrate on the ball and not the sun. If you are playing against a net rusher, send up a high lob when he has the sun in his face. If you are lobbed and you can't see the ball, let it bounce. It is better to let the ball bounce than swing at something you can't see.

In hot, sunny climates dress in cool loose-fitting clothes and wear a hat or visor. Wipe off all perspiration during changeovers and drink plenty of fluids to avoid dehydration. Water is an excellent replacement fluid.

THE CHANGEOVER

During a tournament the players get ninety seconds rest after every odd game. What should you do with this time? Before the early seventies when there were no chairs on the court the players often didn't take the full time. But now that the players can sit down they tend to use it all, and the television stations show a commercial.

You as a player should use this time not only to dry yourself and drink fluids but to think about the match. Think about what you should concentrate on in the upcoming two games. Don't confuse yourself with a lot of different thoughts, keep it simple. For instance, 'I must concentrate more on my first service in the next game,' or if you are the receiver, 'I must play a little higher over the net and go crosscourt because I made too many unforced errors before.'

Even if your opponent is already waiting on the other side, take your time. Don't hurry because your opponent wants you to. Perhaps he has a dental appointment but you don't. Never let yourself be pressured, especially at the beginning of a match when the timing between you and your opponent is being set. Remember, there is always a little psychological warfare going on here.

You should have set your game plan at the beginning of the match. If it is working well then keep to it and concentrate on tactics. Did you win the points or did your opponent make mistakes? Has your opponent changed his or her game plan? Stay alert and if necessary be prepared to adjust your tactics too. It could happen, for example, that your opponent's weak backhand suddenly starts working well. You may have played to it so much that it is now becoming stronger.

WARMING UP BEFORE A MATCH WITH YOUR OPPONENT

Get settled quickly, relax, and concentrate on the upcoming match. Watch the ball, get your timing right and breathe normally. Get a good feel for the ball, try a couple of smashes, lobs and services. Aim at a couple of spots and see how your opponent is playing. If you don't know him, check his strong points and his weaknesses. See how he reacts to fast, slow, high, low and spin balls.

Show him that you are confident even if you are not. He cannot see the butterflies in your stomach. Keep the psychological edge.

PLAYING DOUBLES

To be successful in doubles you need to have a good all-round game that includes all the key shots. You should be consistent in your serving and returning and able to create an opening. You need good spin services, good low returns of service, good volleys and quick reflexes. And not only should you have these shots but the partner you choose should have them too.

On top of that you and your partner must think on the same wavelength and act as a team on the court. You must be aggressive together, anticipate together and cooperate. You must understand each other's movements. You must be able to accept that although you might set up all the points your partner may get the glory for the winning shot. This mutual understanding is especially important because in doubles you have to accept not only your mistakes but also your partner's. During the match, if your partner is having a bad day you have to try even harder. If you are used to playing singles it can be difficult to adopt this cooperative team spirit.

Doubles tactics are a little more complicated than singles tactics. There is more need to anticipate, to move instinctively at the right moment, and there is more variation of shots and more short angled shots. In singles you have to try to hit deep with a good margin over the net, while in doubles you have to try to hit lower over the net making the ball land at the feet of the incoming opponent. There has to be total cooperation between partners. You need to know where your partner is at all times. Both at the net and at the baseline, the partners should move together as if attached by an invisible cord. And you need to play in the same manner at the same time. You should be aggressive together. If you are attacking, your partner should not stand flatfooted watching the game from a distance. Or if you are at the net your partner should come in as well to form a team with you. Always try to get to the net before your opponents. Play at their feet so that they have to lift the ball over the net. You and your partner will then be right on top to hit something away for a winner. You need to know exactly what kind of

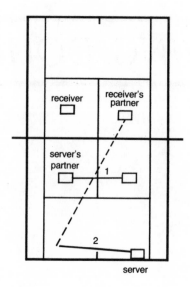

DIAGRAM 32

Playing together at the net gives a better defence.

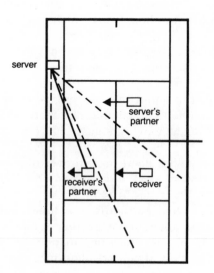

DIAGRAM 33

Partners should always move together as if attached by an invisible cord.

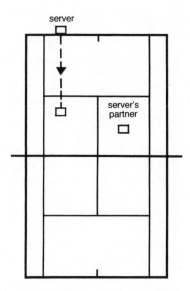

DIAGRAM 34

By standing further away from the centre mark the server has a shorter route to the net and can cope better with any sharply angled crosscourt returns.

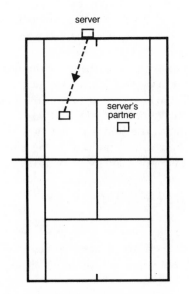

DIAGRAM 35

By standing closer to the centre mark the server has more ground to cover to reach the net.

shots your partner usually plays, how he plans for the point and how he solves certain game situations. You should set the point up together so that one player can finish it.

This teamwork can be achieved by mutual understanding, by talking or by signals. Whatever method you decide to use, make sure it is arranged in advance so as to avoid misunderstanding and unnecessary collisions on the court. Always try to make your partner aware of what you are about to do or what you think they or the opposing team are about to do. It may be necessary to talk during the point. For example if a lob is coming over the centre of the court, call out to make clear who you expect to take the ball. 'Yours' is often heard in doubles. Or if you cross to your partner's side of the net, call out 'switch' if you don't think your partner will move automatically to the other side of the court. The changeover is an excellent time to talk to your partner. If you are both uptight you can help each other to calm down or you can talk strategy for the coming points. One time in Stuttgart I was playing doubles with Pam Shriver and during the changeover I asked Pam: 'When do we get new balls?' Pam totally misunderstood me and replied, 'Yes, Hana, you are the boss.' When I repeated what I had asked her we both laughed so hard and so long that we had trouble concentrating on the next point. Fortunately we recovered and went on to win the tournament.

Make sure you understand each other well and keep your word. If you say that you are going to poach on the next service on the backhand, then go ahead and do it. Your partner needs to know for sure that you are going to keep your word, otherwise you will both end up in the same half of the court making life very easy for your opponent. It will be some time before all the kinks are ironed out, but the most important thing is to keep communicating with each other. communicating with each other.

The better you get to know your partner's style of play, the better you will work together as a team. You will learn to anticipate your partner's movements and shots and this will give you more time to set up your own shots and to gain valuable court space to make better shots. This cooperation and teamwork won't all come in the first few matches. It takes time and a lot of hard work but eventually you will build a strong and successful partnership together and you will also get a lot more pleasure out of the game.

SERVING AND RECEIVING

The service, return of service, volley and smash are the shots most used in doubles. The service and return of service together account for about 50 per cent of the strokes. Let's look a little more closely at the basic positions in doubles.

The Server

Divide the court into four. The server has one quarter to take care of. He starts the point and can dictate the kind of point that will be played. The

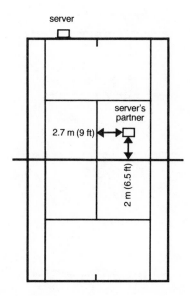

DIAGRAM 36

The server's partner should stand approximately 2 m (6.6 ft) from the net and 2.7 m (8.8 ft) from the centre serviceline.

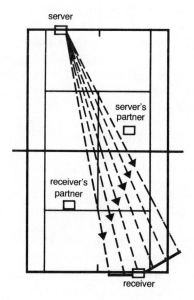

DIAGRAM 37

The position of the receiver from which he can return both on the forehand and the backhand.

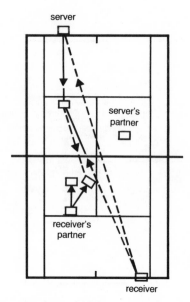

DIAGRAM 38

The position of the receiver's partner from which he can move into the net to take the first volley. The exact direction he moves will depend on what kind of service was played.

server should stand about 2 metres (6.5 feet) from the centre mark on the baseline. That way the rest of his quarter will not be left too open and the receiver will have less space into which he can hit the ball. Also, the server will not have to run as far to cover a sharp-angled crosscourt return and will be able to take a shorter route to the net (see Diagrams 34 and 35).

The best service to use in doubles is a hard service with spin, placed to the receiver's backhand. The spin will go higher over the net and give the server more time to move into the net. Returning this service from the deuce-court is very difficult. The ball jumps oddly and, on the backhand, it is almost impossible to hit down the line.

The Server's Partner

The server's partner should stand so that he is already in an attacking position, at the net. Don't stand too close or you may be lobbed. But on the other hand stand close enough to hit a volley on a weak return. The ideal position is in the centre of the servicecourt, about 2 metres (6.5 feet) from the net and 2.7 metres (9 feet) from the centre serviceline. This position will also depend somewhat on the player's height and mobility.

The Receiver

The receiver of the service should stand so that he is able to return both on the forehand and the backhand. After the return of service the receiver should move immediately to the net. Exactly how far forward he should move depends on what kind of return he played. Ideally the return should be a low crosscourt shot to the server's feet which the netman can't reach.

The Receiver's Partner

The receiver's partner should stand on the serviceline in the centre of his quarter of the court. After the return of service he should move two steps forward and be ready to volley a weak first volley of the server. If the receiver did a good job of playing the return to the server's feet, the receiver's partner should be able to step in and play a winning volley. In doubles 75 per cent of.the points are won at the net which shows how important it is to have a good volley.

OFFENSIVE AND DEFENSIVE POSITIONS

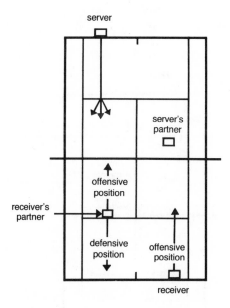

DIAGRAM 39

The server has a good service and both he and his partner have good volleys. He should go to the net after his service.

The receiver has gone to the net after the return of service. The receiver's partner should move forward to intercept a weak volley by the server.

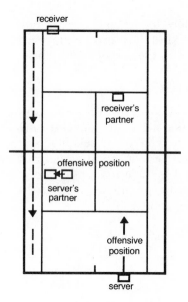

DIAGRAM 40

The receiver has passed the server's partner down the line several times with good winning shots. The server's partner should move closer to the sideline to force the receiver to hit a crosscourt return. The server should join his partner at the net after his service.

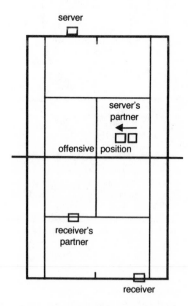

DIAGRAM 41

The receiver is not using the down the line return. The server's partner should move a step closer to the middle to put pressure on the crosscourt return. This will force the receiver to make sharper angled shots and he will be less likely to make a good return.

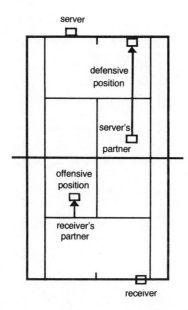

DIAGRAM 42

The server has a weak and predictable service. The server's partner should move back to the baseline, wait until the return has been played and then move in after a short ball. In this case the receiver's partner should move two steps forward on the service.

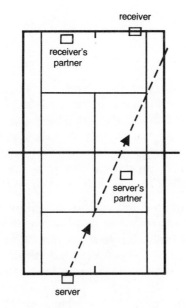

DIAGRAM 43

The server has a very strong service and the receiver is having trouble returning it consistently and low. The receiver's partner should stand on the baseline during the return and both players should move in together on a short ball.

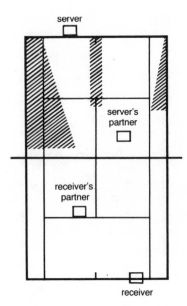

DIAGRAM 44

After a good service the server should move in, otherwise the receiver will be in a good offensive position to play back to the marked spots, and this will give problems to the server.

THE LOB

As I said at the beginning of this chapter, a doubles team should move together as if they were attached by an invisible cord. The offensive and defensive positions should be balanced. That is, the team should either be together at the net or together back at the baseline. It is important to agree beforehand on who is going to take which shots. Keep the agreement otherwise there will be confusion and the thrust of the partnership will be lost. Who should take the lob? Let's look at the different possibilities.

1. Both players are at the net and you are lobbed over your head. Either you agree that you will take *all* your own lobs or that your partner will run after your lobs. It is easier for your partner to run after your lob because he does not have to turn 180 degrees, and at the same time as he runs he can keep an eye on where the opposition is. You, as netplayer, should make a switch to the other side.
2. Your partner is on his way to the net and you are at the net already. You are being lobbed either over your head or over your partner's head. Under these circumstances you should go after the lob because it would be too difficult for your partner, who is running forward, to stop and make a full turn to retrieve it. It would also take him much longer. Make

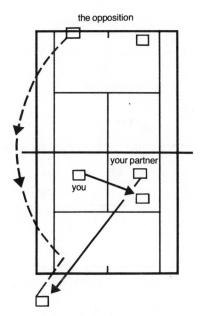

DIAGRAM 45

1. You are both at the net. Your partner runs to take the lob and you switch sides.

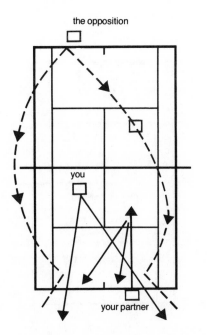

DIAGRAM 46

2. You run back to take the lob because it would take too long for your partner who is running forward to stop and make a full turn.

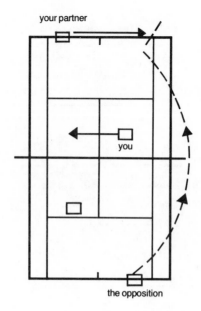

DIAGRAM 47

3. Your partner plays back the lob from the baseline while you switch sides.

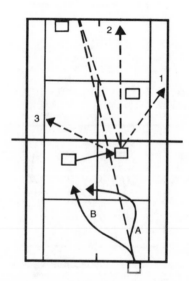

DIAGRAM 48

Poaching: 'A' is the path to follow when you know the net player is going to poach and 'B' is the path to follow when the net player poaches unexpectedly. Aim the volley winner at '1', '2' or '3'.

sure you throw back a good high defensive lob that will give you and
your partner time to form a balanced team again.
3. The third possibility is that your partner is not coming to the net at all.
He does not like to volley and intends to stay at the baseline. In this case,
when you are lobbed over your head, your partner should play back the
lob while you move to the other half of the court.

POACHING

Poaching usually occurs when one player is at the baseline and the other is
at the net. To play good doubles at the net you have to learn to intercept
any ball coming over on your partner's side, which you may be able to
volley for a winner. At the net you have the best opportunity to finish the
point, and the closer you are the easier it becomes, because the more you
can angle your shots.

When crossing to your partner's side make sure you step diagonally
towards the net. If you move parallel to it the shot becomes much more
difficult. As soon as the opponent has made a commitment to his shot, take
off for your poach. Don't hesitate when you poach. And when you go, *go all
the way*. Cross over to your partner's half. Your partner should take your
side.

Always poach if possible on the return of service as it will put pressure
on the returner and may cause him to lose his stroke. If you are the returner
and the other side keeps poaching, throw up a lob over the netplayer's
head.

I-FORMATION OR AUSTRALIAN FORMATION

Partners who have played together for a long time and who understand
each other well might consider using the I-formation (also called the
Australian formation). In this formation, after the service, the net player
moves immediately across to the server's side.

This formation is an excellent way to upset the return of service, especially
when the receiver has an outstanding crosscourt return because he will
now be forced to hit hard down the line and in doing so may well make
mistakes.

Please note that only a pair who have played together for a long time
should try the I-formation. The server has a much greater distance to cover
to the open court for his first volley, and if he is not fast enough he may
have to take it low and play the ball up.

If the server decides to play a wide serve on the deuce-court the
I-formation will not work, because the net player cannot go over to intercept
with a volley. The surprise element is gone.

It is best to serve down the middle to the opponent's backhand on the
deuce-court and wide to the opponent's backhand on the ad-court. In that

case, even if the receiver knows that the serve is coming to his backhand, he still has to hit the return not knowing where the net player will move after the service.

CHOOSING A PARTNER

When playing doubles it is very important to choose the right partner. You will all have much more fun, including your opponents, if you are about the same standard. It would be good to have a partner who is a stronger player than you but then they, in turn, would probably like a stronger partner. In any case, with an equally good partner the team is well balanced and the opponents will not have a target in the weaker player.

Doubles means teamwork, and you have to do all those little things that make a team click. First, you must complement each other in style and temperament. If you are more advanced you should try to match with someone who has strokes that you lack. For example, if you don't have a good overhead and volley, get someone who is confident at the net and has those strokes. It is also important to play with someone you like. It is no good playing with someone you don't get on with as immediately half the fun is gone and before long you will start to have disagreements. A missed volley on an important point can sometimes do a lot of harm to a relationship if you don't understand each other well.

Be considerate towards your partner. If things are going wrong don't blame your partner. Assume they are doing their best and offer encouragement. Tell your partner when he or she has played a good shot. Talk to each other. Professional players often exchange a few words in the middle of a game as they prepare for the next point.

Who should play on which side? A lot of people think that the player with the best forehand should play on the forehand side of the court (the deuce-court). I don't agree with that because the majority of balls come down the centre of the court. If one player's forehand really is stronger then they should play on the backhand side of the court (the ad-court).

From the forehand side of the court the return is often more difficult because the server will place the ball right through the middle of the court, on the receiver's backhand. A backhand return crosscourt from there is an awkward shot to make and it is very difficult to play to the feet of the incoming server. On the backhand side of the court it is more natural to hit the backhand return crosscourt. On top of that, serving to the backhand side or ad-court is more difficult for the server. The net is slightly higher than when serving to the forehand side of the court or deuce-court.

FOUR PLAYERS AT THE NET

When all four players are at the net, after the receiver has made a good low return and the server a good first volley, all is evened out. There are no

When hitting a backhand volley, the backswing should be kept short and knees bent if the ball comes low over the net.

Hana Mandlikova teamed with Chris Evert in the doubles at Wimbledon 1989. Notice the position of each player ready for the point.

advantages or disadvantages to one side or the other.

In this situation the exchange between the four players will be very fast and the point is more likely to be won due to an error rather than by strategy. Hit one ball too high and the opponent will finish the point. The idea is to try and find an opening and then put the ball away.

When four players are at the net it is a good opportunity to try the volley-lob. Never hit the volley-lob when the ball is above the net. In that case it is better to finish the point with an angled shot or one through the middle. Rather, use the volley-lob when the ball is below the net and the opponents are closing in for the volley. The volley-lob is then a real surprise. If you don't execute the shot well, watch out. They may use you as a target ...

MIXED DOUBLES

To play good mixed doubles you should play just as you would in any doubles match. A good female doubles player should not let herself be intimidated by the male player. Play as you would normally — good serving, good returning and good volleying. The man may take a little more of the court, especially in the middle, and a lob through the middle of the court will almost certainly be taken by the man.

Here is a quote from my coach, Betty Stove, on playing mixed doubles: 'I have never been afraid of the man, not even Ion Tiriac, who always tried at the start of a match to hit as hard as possible to the woman to make her afraid. On the contrary, it was a challenge. The man usually thinks that he can overpower you but with good technique and by staying alert you should never be intimidated. If you show that you are afraid and move more to the alley, you make it much more difficult for you and your partner. Just keep playing normal doubles and keep poaching. Keep the man honest and try to pass him down the line a couple of times. My doubles partner, Frew McMillan, and I won many tournaments, including the Wimbledon Championships and the US Open Championships. He always made me feel comfortable beside him and encouraged me to poach often.'

TRAINING

My first trainer was my father. His own background was very athletic and he determined to make a good athlete out of me. He gave me a good healthy base for the sport and I am very grateful for the values he instilled in me.

However, despite his years of care and attention, I haven't always been as fit as I should be. Some years ago, when I had just started on the women's protour, my coach Betty showed me that I could have won a match if only I had been in better shape. I lost 6–4 4–6 6–4 and during the third set I became really tired. It was then I realized, for the first time, that I was not in the great physical shape I should have been in for professional tennis. During the match I slowly lost my concentration and played a couple of short balls. I know that if I had been fitter I would have been able to return those balls properly.

As you really start to enjoy tennis, either because of the pleasure and exercise offered by friendly competition or because of tournament success, you will find that it is necessary to pay more attention to your physical shape. Success, especially in more advanced tennis, depends not only on what you do on the court during the actual match, but also on what you have done to prepare yourself before you go on court. To get the best out of yourself it is very important that besides playing tennis you get your body and mind into top shape. The qualities that are essential to good tennis include:

- Power
- Speed
- Stamina
- Flexibility
- Coordination

This looks like an awful lot, and of course on top of that you must have some feeling for ball games, but all these things together, along with many hours of hard work, will eventually make you into a top player.

The human body is a miracle. It can do the most incredible amount of hard work and then recuperate to its original state. But the time necessary to recuperate depends entirely on the state of your physical condition. A few simple facts: the body needs energy and this is provided by oxygen and glucose. Air provides the oxygen, to the lungs, which is then distributed in the muscles by the pumping of the heart. And this process can be improved by physical exercise.

In tennis the importance of physical fitness cannot be underestimated. A powerful service, a net attack and a strong baseline rally all require good physical condition. In order to have the motivation to learn better technique and tactics you must be fit. And the stamina to achieve power, speed, quick reactions, mobility and agility also depends on your physical fitness.

Tennis training and physical fitness training are now much more specialized. Top players usually vary their training programs according to whether they are playing a tournament or not. During a tournament I would not recommend doing much physical training. Most tennis training sessions include physical movements with the tennis ball anyway. However, whatever the day, stretching or warming up should always be on your schedule.

WARMING UP

Before you start any training you should always do a proper warming up routine. That way you will avoid the risk of injury and you will also play better. The muscles, joints and ligaments should be made warm and supple. You will then feel more relaxed and able to concentrate better on the timing of the perfect ball.

Always start with skipping or running to get the blood pumping through the whole body. Then stretch the muscles you use in tennis. These include the shoulders, arms, groin, quadriceps, hamstrings, calf muscles, stomach, feet and ankles. Stretch each muscle and hold it in position for twenty seconds. Relax and repeat again three to four times.

Your warming up should take at least fifteen minutes. Make sure you stay warm while you are waiting to start the match or practice session. The effects of warming up wear off after about ten minutes. Keep yourself warm and watch the clock.

OVERALL FITNESS

Before you start specific tennis training drills you need to be in an overall good physical shape. When you embark on a program of physical fitness you need to start slowly and carefully. Set your goals according to your own needs and capabilities. Everybody would like to be a good player but the physical demands of each person are different. However, the benefits of good physical condition are universal. A healthy fit body can take more pain, recuperate faster and move more quickly. Plus, the mind inside will be more motivated and able to concentrate better.

The level of physical fitness is determined in each case by the individual character. For the club player, the level of normal physical condition should give the player stamina, power, speed and flexibility. For the top player top shape is an absolute must.

Start with some basic training. Go running slowly, twice a day, for fifteen minutes. Try to run so that you can still speak. Build this up slowly until you can run with ease and don't run on stone or asphalt. The muscles, joints and tendons will get stronger and their flexibility will improve. When you have a good base with good recovery you can start interval-training. To do this you should run at 80 per cent of your normal speed and then rest by jogging slowly.

For example:

1. Run 15 seconds.
   Rest 15 seconds.
   Repeat 20–30 times.
2. Run 1 minute.
   Rest 15 seconds.
   Repeat 10 times.
3. Run 4 minutes.
   Rest 2 minutes.
   Repeat 5 times.

Once you have reached a decent fitness level by training twice a day, you can maintain good physical condition by training longer at least twice a week. To become a top player you need to train five to six times a week. How high you set your goals is up to you.

SPECIFIC TENNIS DRILLS

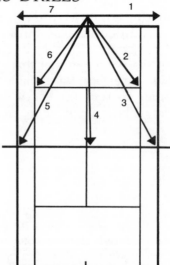

Fan Drill   DIAGRAM 49

Stand on the centre of the baseline with your racquet in hand. Run to every corner, as indicated by the numbers, as fast as possible. Run as you would during a match, sidestepping to the side and backwards from the net.

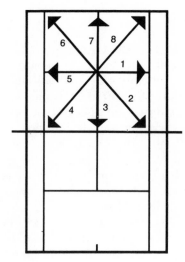

DIAGRAM 50

Star Drill

Start in the middle and run to every corner as fast as possible. Run as you would during a match, sidestepping to the side and backwards from the net.

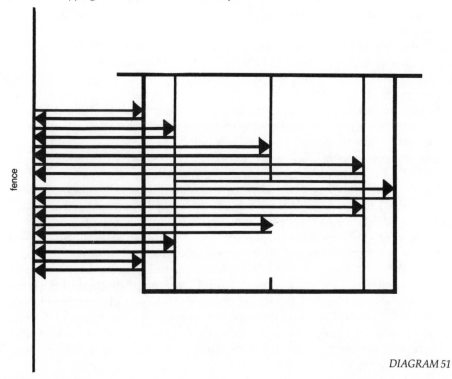

DIAGRAM 51

Killer Drill

Sprint to every line as fast as you can, keeping your weight forward. Touch the lines bending at the knees, not from the waist.

AVOIDING INJURY

In order to avoid injury you must be sure to warm up properly every time before you start to play. Your muscles are cold and you need to get your circulation going. As a youngster you are naturally supple but the older you get the longer it takes to warm up. I believe that young or old, you should do stretching exercises every morning. If you look at an animal which has been sleeping, the first thing it does on waking is stretch itself. We should take an example from this.

Always listen to your body carefully and don't overdo it. When children are young they are usually enthusiastic and want to play and play. Their parents may see a new star in them and push them higher and higher without really knowing what they are doing. They become blinded by the glory that shines on them as well and even see big dollar signs in the future. However, putting such strain on young growing bones can do a lot of harm. Before you reach the top you will need to do many, many hours of practise and your body will have to take a lot more strain. If you overdo it at an early age you could jeopardize your chances for the future. You should also be wary of playing above your age group. The body may not be ready for it. Remember too, that when you progress to a more advanced racquet you will hit the ball harder and your body must be ready to absorb this greater impact.

At the beginning of the book I spoke about tennis as being first and foremost a sport, a means of fun and relaxation. Make sure you keep the fun in the game and don't put pressure on yourself at too young an age. Play other sports. This will be good for your muscle development and stop one side of your body becoming more developed that the other. It will also be good for your game sense and your reaction development.

Do take care of yourself when something is wrong. If you have an unusual strain or pain don't wait too long before going to a knowledgeable doctor. You only have one body and parts of it are not replaceable.

I guess you could say I had to learn the hard way about injuries. When I was young I took a lot of things for granted. But I soon realized that with only half a body I could not play as well. During my career I have had a lot of little injuries. Some I could play on with, some I had to stop for. Now that I know my body much better I know when to go on and when to stop. During the 1980 season I suffered with my back. I kept on playing with it for six months, always thinking it would eventually disappear the same way it had come. Finally I could take the pain no longer and decided to take a good rest and find out exactly what was wrong. A fine doctor in Toronto gave me, after thorough tests, a set of exercises for my lower back. To this day, nine years later, I am still doing those exercises and my back hasn't bothered me once.

DIET

These days everyone talks about dieting. You can't turn on the television without having to hear another expert's views on diet.

In my mind diet is more a habit. If you want to change your diet to lose or gain weight you have to to change your habits. Habits are started from the day you are born. You will usually find that when parents are in good shape their kids are too and when parents are obese their children are also obese. My father, Vilda, was 100-metre (100-yard) champion of Czechoslovakia for eleven years and twice went to the Olympics. He also chose the right person to marry because my mother, Hana, is the best cook in the world. During all those years when she had to cook for my father before and during heavy training seasons she knew exactly what was good for him. She always served a hot tasty meal twice a day and to this day I try to eat two hot meals a day. Mother taught me not only what to include in a nutritious balanced diet but also how to make it appetizing. The whole family did well on her cooking and we were always full of energy.

Food gives us energy and the materials with which to grow and tune our muscle tissue. It also gives us the various essential vitamins and minerals which our body needs to function. The body always needs energy. Even when you are sleeping you use energy to keep your heart, lungs and organs going and to keep your normal body temperature. The more active you are, the more kilojoules (or calories) you burn up, and the more you have to eat in order to replace then, for more energy. Also, a heavy person burns up more energy than a light person.

It follows from all this that if you wish to lose weight, you have to burn up more energy than you replace. In other words, you have to exercise more and eat less. A very active player should consume more kilojoules (calories) a day than the average person, depending on their height and build. However, these extra kilojoules (calories) should come from the right kind of food. A piece of cake with a nice topping is not the right kind of food.

Your daily diet should consist of 60 per cent carbohydrates, 25 per cent fat and 15 per cent protein. One gram (0.035 oz) of carbohydrate produces 16 kJ (4 Cals) of energy, 1 gram (0.035 oz) of fat produces 37 kJ (9 Cals) of energy and 1 gram (0.035 oz) of protein produces 17 kJ (4 Cals) of energy. Younger people people who are still growing need more protein and vitamins. Here is a breakdown of what an active tennis player should consume daily:

Milk, buttermilk or yoghurt (vitamin B); one of these with every meal.
Potatoes and pasta, vegetables and fruits (vitamin C); all three at some
    stage during the day.
Cheese, meat, fish, eggs or leguminous plants (vitamin B); cheese and one
    or more of the others every day.
Butter or margarine (vitamin A); a little every day.
Brown bread, pumpernickel or muesli (vitamin B_1); bread and/or muesli
    every day.

Try to eat a variety of foods and never overeat. You should always leave the table with the feeling that you could eat more. Ideally, your daily allowance should be consumed over five meals. Here is a sample menu:

Breakfast :   fruit or fruit juice
              muesli with milk or yoghurt
10.30 :   1 or 2 slices brown bread with cheese or meat
              tea or milk
Lunch :   spaghetti with a light sauce
              salad and fruit
3.30 :   tea, milk or yoghurt
              1 slice brown bread (if hungry)
Dinner :   soup
              75 grams (2.5 oz) meat or fish, or 2 eggs
              5 spoonfuls vegetables, salad and potatoes
              fruit or yoghurt

What an athlete eats is important but unfortunately there is no magic diet which can guarantee you win the match. You only become a better player by training. However the wrong food can influence your results detrimentally. Not everybody should eat the same food. Diet is an individual matter. If you want to be a top player you should talk to a dietician who will be able to determine what is good for *your* body.

Eat at least two hours before you play but not too much otherwise the blood will have to work so hard at digesting the food it will not be able to help your muscles supply the energy you need to play. I try to eat at least three hours before my match. Sometimes that is difficult to figure out as the matches before can last longer than expected so I have to eat little bites to satisfy my stomach. Usually I have some cold cooked spaghetti salad in my bag which I can nibble on.

It is good to drink a lot of water during the day and during your matches. Drink a little all the time. If you have perspired a lot during a game drink plenty of milk, fruit juice or bouillon to replenish the salt, minerals and iron lost. I do not recommend carbonated drinks. They are usually very cold and draw extra blood for their digestion away from the muscles. They may also give you an upset stomatch. Now and then an evening glass of beer won't do you any harm and can be very relaxing.

THE PSYCHE TO WIN

The psychology of a tennis match is very interesting, and not that difficult to understand. But before you try to understand the workings of your opponent's mind make sure you understand yourself. You should know how you react under different circumstances, how you feel when conditions are changing around you and how well you can control yourself. If you know yourself and your own reactions then you are in a position to study the thoughts and temperament of your opponent.

There are basically four kinds of players. In the first category is the player who stands on the baseline and just hits the ball back without any strategy at all. The second kind of player is also a baseline player, but he tries to outmanoeuvre his opponent and break up his game. The idea is to catch his opponent out with a short ball or a high ball from the baseline. This kind of player always has a plan and will stick to it. The third kind of player is the serve and volley player. He is usually an impulsive sort of person who acts on instinct rather than according to any plan. He can make some fantastic shots and the crowd adore him but he lacks consistency. If only he would put a little more thought into his game he would be brilliant. The fourth and most dangerous kind of player is the total player. This is the player who can mix a strong baseline game with an aggressive net attack. He is always alert as to what is going on and he has a solid game plan which he goes after.

When two players of about the same standard play the same type of game, then the edge will probably lie with the player who has the mental authority in the game. Remember, luck always goes with the winner. At least that's what the loser thinks anyway.

In a tennis match both players start from zero. If one player gets a lead, his whole purpose will be to keep that lead and if he does he will keep his confidence. The opponent, on the other hand, will be worried and his mental outlook lowered. However, if he should manage to make the score even, he will then have the psychological edge. He will be in a very positive frame of mind and thinking about winning, while the player who was first ahead will now have had a drop in confidence and be trying to psych himself back into the game. It is this change in psychology that can make a player, who was very far behind, end up winning.

Of course it is extremely difficult when you are very far behind to climb back and win the match. That is why it is so important, if you have an early lead, to keep your concentration and motivation going. Stay in control, and whatever you do, don't start worrying that the situation might change. This will only take your mind off the actual point in hand. To play to the score is very important. Two very important points in the game are the third and fourth points, that is 15−15 or 30−15. On these the server should work very hard. If you are the server and the service games are getting longer and longer, don't start worrying. By worrying you will only increase the nervous tension of the match and make it harder for yourself.

We discussed earlier the tactics and significance of various point scores (*see p. 72*). Let's now look at some game score situations. You have just broken your opponent's service and you are 3−1 ahead and serving. This is a very dangerous situation because unconsciously you might let up for the next game, thinking you already have a two-game lead. The opponent, meanwhile, will be fighting back to break your service. And if you lose that game the score will be 3−2 and it could well go to 3−3 if your opponent holds his service. So now, instead of being 5−1 or 4−2 ahead, you are only even. Never relax your attack before the last ball has been played.

Another dangerous situation is when the score is 5−2. In this case the losing player may look like he is beaten — after all there is not much more to lose and he might as well relax — but at the same time he will make one final bid to win. And you don't know what to expect. Maybe he will attack strongly or maybe he will concentrate on avoiding his unforced errors. On the other hand he might start playing dropshots and lobs. Or even something else. At the same time you may be thinking, 'Oh, I've already won this match,' or you might be getting a little too correct or a little too relaxed. (This is when it is important to know yourself.) And then before you know, it will be 5—4 and your only service break advantage gone. To win the match now you would have to make a break. So you see how it can be — from a 5—2 lead to a 7—5 defeat in no time.

How do you avoid these traps? I think the best strategy is to continue playing as you have been and not let anything else slip into your mind. So, instead of letting up, concentrate on taking the ball earlier and put more pressure on your opponent so that his attack is put down immediately. He will then think that if you are going to keep pushing forward as you are, he will have no chance in the second set either.

If your opponent should hit a great shot, drawing a lot of applause, remind yourself that it only counts for one point. Give him credit for it but at the same time forget it. Go on with the game. If you keep thinking about it you may lose the next two points as well. Never lose your temper when your opponent hits a good shot. It is bad enough losing it over your own bad shots. And never lose your temper over a bad decision by the umpire.

The object of tennis is to win. And you can win by breaking up your opponent's game. This is all part of good tactics and for you it means staying in control under all circumstances. Another part of good tactics is to concentrate on your opponent's weakness. Keep hitting at it and hitting at it until it breaks down. If your opponent then loses his confidence and shows it, you have him where you want him. Know your opponent and make your game plan accordingly. If he loves a target at the net, stay on the baseline. If he expects you to stay back, come in to the net. If he attacks, attack back. He will then be busy fighting your attack and his own attack will suffer. The best defence is an offence. If he is a steady player do not try to beat him at his own game. In most cases he will be better at it. Try instead to hit winners and go to the net. However if your opponent plays irregularly and misses a lot of shots, keep the ball in play and let him make the mistakes. Slowly his confidence will decrease.

Remember, never change a winning game. However you should always change a losing game and in this case the question is when. If you lost the first set 6—4 or 6—3, with only one service break, yes, you lost the set, but you should not change your game just because of one service game. However, if you lost the first set 6—1 or 6—2 it is time to change.

Take chances when you are behind but never when you are ahead. Taking risks only pays off when you are down and have everything to gain and nothing to lose. Fight all the time and smile sometimes. It will boost your confidence and may confuse your opponent. Let everybody know that you play for the pleasure of it. You will find the game much easier and more enjoyable.

APPENDIX — RULES OF TENNIS

THE SINGLES GAME

RULE 1

The court shall be a rectangle of 78 feet (23.77 m) long and 27 feet (8.23 m) wide.

It shall be divided across the middle by a net suspended from a cord or metal cable, the end of which shall be attached to, or pass over, the tops of two posts. The centres of the posts shall be 3 feet (0.914 m) outside the court on each side and the height of the posts shall be such that the top of the cord or metal cable shall be 3 feet 6 inches (1.07 m) above ground.

When a combined doubles (see Rule 34) and singles court with a doubles net is used for singles, the net must be supported to a height of 3 feet 6 inches (1.07 m) by means of two posts, called "singles sticks".

The net shall be extended fully so that it fills completely the space between the two posts and shall be of sufficiently small mesh to prevent the ball passing through. The height of the net shall be 3 feet (0.914 m) at the centre, where it shall be held down taut by a strap.

The lines bounding the ends and sides of the Court shall respectively be called the Base-lines and the Side-lines. On each side of the net, at a distance of 21 feet (6.40 m) from it and parallel with it, shall be drawn the Service-lines. The space on each side of the net between the service-line and the side-lines shall be divided into two equal parts called the service courts by the centre service-line, drawn half-way between, and parallel with the side-lines.

RULE 2

The permanent fixtures of the court shall include not only the net, posts, singles sticks, cord or metal cable, strap and band, but also, where there are any, the back and side stops, the stands, fixed or movable seats and chairs around the Court and their occupants, all other fixtures around and above the Court, and the Umpire, Net Cord Judge, Foot Fault Judge, Linesmen and Ball Boys when in their places.

RULE 3

The ball shall have a uniform outer surface and shall be white or yellow in colour. If there are any seams they shall be stitchless.

RULE 4   *The Racket*

Rackets failing to comply with the following specifications are not approved for play under the Rules of Tennis:

(a) The hitting surface of the racket shall be flat and consist of a pattern of crossed strings connected to a frame and alternately interfaced or bonded where they cross; and the stringing pattern shall be generally uniform, and in particular not less dense in the centre than in any other area. The strings shall be free of attached objects and protrusions other than those utilised solely and specifically to limit or prevent wear and tear or vibration and which are reasonable in size and placement for such purposes.

(b) The frame of the racket shall not exceed 32 inches (81.28 cm) in overall length, including the handle, and 12½ inches (31.75 cm) in overall width. The strung surface shall not exceed 15½ inches (39.37 cm) in overall length, and 11½ inches (29.21 cm) in overall width.

(c) The frame, including the handle, shall be free of attached objects and devices other than those utilised solely and specifically to limit or prevent wear and tear or vibration, or to distribute weight. Any objects and devices must be reasonable in size and placement for such purposes.

(d) The frame, including the handle and the strings, shall be free of any device which makes it possible to change materially the shape of the racket, or to change the weight distribution, during the playing of a point.

RULE 5

The players shall stand on opposite sides of the net; the player who first delivers the ball shall be called the Server, and the other the Receiver.

RULE 6

The choice of ends and the right to be Server or Receiver in the first game shall be decided by toss.

The player winning the toss may choose, or require his opponent to choose:

(a) The right to be Server or Receiver, in which case the other player shall choose the end; or

(b) The end, in which case the other player shall choose the right to be Server or Receiver.

RULE 7

The service shall be delivered in the following manner: Immediately before commencing to serve, the Server shall stand with both feet at rest behind (i.e. further from the net than) the base-line and within the imaginary continuations of the centre-mark and side-line. The Server shall then project the ball by hand into the air in any direction and before it hits the ground strike it with his racket, and the delivery shall be deemed to have been completed at the moment of the impact of the racket and the ball.

RULE 8

(a) The Server shall throughout the delivery of the

service:

(i) Not change his position by walking or running. The Server shall not by slight movements of the feet, which do not materially affect the location originally taken up by him, be deemed "to change his position by walking or running".

(ii) Not touch, with either foot, any area other than that behind the base-line within the imaginary extension of the centre mark and side-lines.

(b) The word "foot" means the extremity of the leg below the ankle.

RULE 9

(a) In delivering the service, the Server shall stand alternately behind the right and left Courts, beginning from the right in every game. If service from a wrong half of the Court occurs and is undetected, all play resulting from such wrong service or services shall stand, but the inaccuracy of station shall be corrected immediately it is discovered.

(b) The ball served shall pass over the net and hit the ground within the Service Court which is diagonally opposite, or upon any line bounding such Court, before the Receiver returns it.

RULE 10

The service is a fault:

(a) If the Server commits any breach of Rules 7, 8 or 9;

(b) If he misses the ball in attempting to strike it;

(c) If the ball served touches a permanent fixture (other than the net, strap or band) before it hits the ground.

RULE 11

After a fault (if it is the first fault) the Server shall serve again from behind the same half of the Court from which he served that fault, unless the service was from the wrong half, when, in accordance with Rule 9, the Server shall be entitled to one service only from behind the other half.

RULE 12

The Server shall not serve until the Receiver is ready. If the latter attempts to return the service he shall be deemed ready. If, however, the Receiver signifies that he is not ready he may not claim a fault because the ball does not hit the ground within the limits fixed for the service.

RULE 13

In all cases where a let has to be called under the rules, or to provide for an interruption to play, it shall have the following interpretation:

(a) When called solely in respect of a service, that one service only shall be replayed;

(b) When called under any other circumstances, the point shall be replayed.

RULE 14

The service is a let:

(a) If the ball served touches the net, strap or band, and is otherwise good, or, after touching the net, strap or band, touches the Receiver or anything which he wears or carries, before hitting the ground;

(b) If a service or a fault is delivered when the Receiver is not ready (see Rule 12). In case of a let, that particular service shall not count, and the Server shall serve again, but a service let does not annul a previous fault.

RULE 15

At the end of the first game the Receiver shall become Server, and the Server Receiver, and so on alternately in all the subsequent games of a match.

If a player serves out of turn, the player who ought to have served shall serve as soon as the mistake is discovered, but all points scored before such a discovery shall be reckoned. A fault served before such a discovery shall not be reckoned. If a game is completed before such a discovery, the order of service remains as altered.

RULE 16

The players shall change ends at the end of the first, third and every subsequent alternate game of each set, and at the end of each set, unless the total number of games in a set is even, in which case the change is not made until the end of the first game of the next set.

If a mistake is made and the correct sequence is not followed the players must take up their correct station as soon as the discovery is made and follow their original sequence.

RULE 17

A ball is in play from the moment at which it is delivered in service. Unless a fault or a let is called it remains in play until the point is decided.

RULE 18

The Server wins the point:

(a) If the ball served, not being a let under Rule 14, touches the Receiver or anything which he wears or carries, before it hits the ground;

(b) If the Receiver otherwise loses the point as provided by Rule 20.

RULE 19

The Receiver wins the point: (a) If the Server serves two consecutive faults; (b) If the Server otherwise loses the point as provided by Rule 20.

RULE 20

A player loses the point if:

(a) He fails, before the ball in play hits the ground twice consecutively, to return it directly over the net (except as provided in Rule 24(a) or (c);

(b) He returns the ball in play so that it hits the ground, a permanent fixture, or other object outside any of the lines which bound his opponent's Court, except as provided in Rule 24(a) and (c);

(c) He volleys the ball and fails to make a good return even when standing outside the Court;

(d) In playing the ball he deliberately carries or catches it on his racket or deliberately touches it with his racket more than once;

(e) He or his racket (in his hand, or otherwise) or anything which he wears or carries, touches the net, posts, singles sticks, cord or metal cable, strap or band, or the ground within his opponent's Court, at any time while the ball is in play;

(f) He volleys the ball before it has passed the net;

(g) The ball in play touches him or anything that he wears or carries, except his racket in his hand or hands;

(h) He throws his racket at and hits the ball;

(i) He deliberately and materially changes the shape of his racket during the playing of the point.

RULE 21

If a player commits any act which hinders his opponent in making a stroke, then, if this is deliberate, he shall lose the point, or if involuntary, the point shall be replayed.

RULE 22

A ball falling on a line is regarded as falling in the Court bounded by that line.

RULE 23

If the ball in play touches a permanent fixture (other than the net, posts, singles stick, cord or metal cable, strap or band) after it has hit the ground, the player who struck it wins the point; if before it hits the ground, his opponent wins the point.

RULE 24

It is a good return:

(a) If the ball touches the net, posts, singles stick, cord or metal cable, strap or band, provided that it passes over any of them and hits the ground within the Court;

(b) If the ball, served or returned, hits the ground within the proper Court, and re-bounds or is blown back over the net, and the player whose turn it is to strike reaches over the net and plays the ball, provided that neither he nor any part of his clothes or racket touches the net, posts, singles stick, cord or metal cable, strap or band or the ground within his opponent's Court, and the stroke is otherwise good;

(c) If the ball is returned outside the post or singles stick either above or below the level of the top of the net, even though it touches the post or singles stick provided that it hits the ground within the proper Court;

(d) If a player's racket passes over the net after he has returned the ball, provided the ball passes the net before being played and is properly returned;

(e) If a player succeeds in returning a ball, served or in play, which strikes a ball lying in the Court.

RULE 25

In case a player is hindered in making a stroke by anything not within his control, except a permanent fixture of the Court or except as provided for in Rule 21, a let shall be called.

RULE 26

If a player wins his first point, the score is called 15 for that player; on winning his second point, the score is called 30 for that player; on winning his third point, the score is called 40 for that player, and the fourth point won by a player is scored game for that player except as below:

If both players have won three points, the score is called deuce; and the next point won by a player is scored advantage for that player. If the same player wins the next point, he wins the game; if the other player wins the next point, the score is again called deuce; and so on until a player wins the two points immediately following the score at deuce, when the game is scored for that player.

RULE 27

(a) A player (or players) who first wins six games wins a set; except that he must win by a margin of two games over his opponent and where necessary a set shall be extended until this margin is achieved.

(b) The tie-break system of scoring may be adopted as an alternative to the advantage set system in paragraph (a) of this Rule provided the decision is announced in advance of the match.

In this case, the following Rules shall be effective:

The tie-break shall operate when the score reaches six games all in any set except in the first set when an ordinary advantage set shall be played, unless otherwise decided and announced in advance of the match.

The following system shall be used in a tie-break game.
Singles

(i) A player who first wins seven points shall win the game and the set, provided he leads by a margin of two points. If the score reaches six points all the game shall be extended until this margin has been achieved. Numerical scoring shall be used throughout the tie-break game.

(ii) The player whose turn it is to serve shall be the server for the first point. His opponent shall be the server for the second and third points and thereafter each player shall alternately serve for two consecutive points until the winner of the game and set has been decided.

(iii) From the first point, each service shall be delivered alternately from the right and left courts, beginning from the right court. If service from a wrong half of the court occurs and is undetected all play resulting from such wrong service or services shall stand but the inaccuracy of station shall be corrected immediately it is discovered.

(iv) Players shall change ends after every six points and at the conclusion of the tie-break game.

(v) The tie-break game shall count as one game for the ball change, except that, if the balls are due to be changed at the beginning of the tie-break, the change shall be delayed until the second game of the following set.

Doubles

In doubles the procedure for singles shall apply. The player whose turn it is to serve shall be the server for the first point. Thereafter each player shall serve in rotation for two points, in the same order as previously in that set, until the winner of the game and set have been decided.

Rotation of Service

The player (or pair in the case of doubles) who served first in the tie-break game shall receive service in the first game of the following set.

RULE 28

The maximum number of sets in a match shall be 5, or where women take part, 3.

RULE 29

In matches where an Umpire is appointed, his decision shall be final; but where a Referee is appointed, an appeal shall lie to him from the decision of an Umpire on a question of law, and in all such cases the decision of the Referee shall be final.

In matches where assistants to the Umpire are appointed (linesmen, net cord judges, foot-fault judges) their decisions shall be final on questions of fact, except that if in the opinion of an Umpire, a clear mistake has been made, he shall have the right to change the decision of an assistant or order a let to be played. When such an assistant is unable to give a decision he shall indicate this immediately to the Umpire who shall give a decision. When an Umpire is unable to give a decision on a question of fact he shall order a let to be played.

In Davis Cup matches or other team competitions where a Referee is on Court, any decision can be changed by the Referee, who may also instruct an Umpire to order a let to be played.

The Referee, at his discretion, may at any time postpone a match on account of darkness or the condition of the ground or the weather. In case of postponement the previous score and previous occupancy of Courts shall hold good, unless the Referee and the players unanimously agree otherwise.

RULE 30

Play shall be continuous from the first service until the match is concluded, in accordance with the following provisions:

(a) If the first service is a fault, the second service must be struck by the Server without delay.

The Receiver must play to the reasonable pace of the Server and must be ready to receive when the Server is ready to serve.

When changing ends a maximum of one minute thirty seconds shall elapse from the moment the ball goes out of play at the end of the game to the time the ball is struck for the first point of the next game.

The Umpire shall use his discretion when there is interference which makes it impractical for play to be continuous.

The organisers of international circuits and team events, recognised by the ITF may determine the time allowed between points, which shall not at any time exceed 30 seconds.

(b) Play shall never be suspended, delayed, or interfered with for the purpose of enabling a player to recover his strength, breath, or physical condition. However, in the case of accidental injury, the Umpire may allow a one-time three minute suspension for that injury. The organisers of international circuits and team events, recognised by the ITF, may extend the one-time suspension period from three minutes to five minutes.

(c) If, through circumstances outside the control of the player, his clothing, footwear, or equipment (excluding racket), becomes out of adjustment in such a way that it is impossible or undesirable for him to play on, the Umpire may suspend play while the maladjustment is rectified.

(d) The Umpire may suspend or delay play at any time as may be necessary and appropriate.

(e) After the third set, or, when women take part, the second set, either player is entitled to a rest, which shall not exceed ten minutes, or in countries situated between latitude 15 degrees north and latitude 15 degrees south, 45 minutes, and furthermore, when necessitated by circumstances not within the control of the players, the Umpire may suspend play for such period as he may consider necessary. If play is suspended, and is not resumed until a later day, the rest may be taken only after the third set, (or when women take part, the second set) of play on such a later day, completion of an unfinished set being counted as one set.

If play is suspended and is not resumed until ten minutes have elapsed in the same day, the rest may be taken only after three consecutive sets have been played without interruption (or when women take part two sets), completion of an unfinished set being counted as one set.

Any nation and/or committee organising a tournament, match, or competition, other than the International Tennis Championships (Davis Cup and Federation Cup), is at liberty to modify this provision, or omit it from its regulations, provided this is announced before the event commences.

(f) A tournament committee has the discretion to decide the time allowed for a warm-up period prior to a match, but this may not exceed five minutes, and must be announced before the event commences.

(g) When approved point penalty and non-accumulative point penalty systems are in operation, the Umpire shall make his decisions within the terms of those systems.

(h) Upon violation of the principle that play shall be continuous the Umpire may, after giving due warning, disqualify the offender.

RULE 31

During the playing of a match in a team competition a player may receive coaching from a Captain who is sitting on the court only when he changes ends at the end of a game, but not when he changes ends during a tie-break game. A player may not receive coaching during the playing of any other match. The provisions of this rule must be strictly construed. After due warning an offending player may be disqualified. When an approved point penalty system is in operation, the Umpire shall impose penalties according to that system.

RULE 32

In cases where balls are to be changed after a specified number of games, if the balls are not changed in the correct sequence the mistake shall be corrected when the player, or pair in the case of doubles, who should have served with the new balls is next due to serve. Thereafter the balls shall be changed so that the number of games between changes shall be that originally agreed.

THE DOUBLES GAME

RULE 33

The above Rules shall apply to the Doubles Game except as below.

RULE 34

For the Doubles Game, the Court shall be 36 feet (10.97 m) in width, i.e. 4½ feet (1.37 m) wider on each side than the Court for the Singles Game.

RULE 35

The order of serving shall be decided at the beginning of each set as follows:

The pair who have to serve in the first game of each set shall decide which partner shall do so, and the opposing pair shall decide similarly for the second game. The partner of the player who served in the first game shall serve in the third; the partner of the player who served in the second game shall serve in the fourth, and so on in the same order in all subsequent games of a set.

RULE 36

The order of receiving the service shall be decided at the beginning of each set as follows:

The pair who have to receive the service in the first game shall decide which partner shall receive the first service, and that partner shall continue to receive the first service in every odd game throughout the set.

The opposing pair shall likewise decide which partner shall receive the first service in the second game, and that partner shall continue to receive the first service in every even game throughout that set.

Partners shall receive the service alternately throughout each game.

RULE 37

If a partner serves out of turn, the partner who ought to have served shall serve as soon as the mistake is discovered, but all points scored and any fault served before such discovery shall be reckoned. If a game is completed before such discovery, the order of service remains as altered.

RULE 38

If during a game the order of receiving the service is changed by the receivers, it shall remain as altered until the end of the game in which the mistake is discovered, but the partners shall resume their original order of receiving in the next game of that set in which they are receivers of the service.

RULE 39

The service is a fault as provided for by Rule 10, or if the ball touches the Server's partner or anything which he wears or carries, but if the ball served touches the partner of the Receiver, or anything which he wears or carries, not being a let under Rule 14(a) before it hits the ground, the Server wins the point.

RULE 40

The ball shall be struck alternately by one or other player of the opposing pairs, and if a player touches the ball in play with his racket in contravention of this Rule, his opponents win the point.

NOTE. Except where otherwise stated every reference in these Rules to the masculine includes the feminine gender.

INDEX